INTRODUCING
MENTAL
HEALTH

—— *A Practical Guide* ——

SECOND EDITION

Caroline Kinsella and Connor Kinsella

Foreword by Vikram Patel

Jessica Kingsley *Publishers*
London and Philadelphia

First Edition published by Jessica Kingsley Publishers in 2006

Second Edition first published in 2015
by Jessica Kingsley Publishers
73 Collier Street
London N1 9BE, UK
and
400 Market Street, Suite 400
Philadelphia, PA 19106, USA

www.jkp.com

Library of Congress Cataloging in Publication Data
Kinsella, Caroline, 1960- , author.
  Introducing mental health : a practical guide / Caroline
Kinsella and Connor Kinsella. -- Second edition.
     p. ; cm.
Includes bibliographical references and indexes.
ISBN 978-1-84905-596-3 (alk. paper)
I. Kinsella, Connor, 1964- , author. II. Title.
[DNLM: 1. Mental Disorders--England--Case Reports.
2. Mental Health--England--Case Reports. WM
140]
 RA790
 362.2--dc23

                              2014047767

British Library Cataloguing in Publication Data
A CIP catalogue record for this book is available from the British Library

ISBN 978 1 84905 596 3
eISBN 978 1 78450 050 4

Printed and bound in the United States

INTRODUCING MENTAL HEALTH

of related interest

The Survival Guide for Newly Qualified Social Workers in Adult and Mental Health Services
Hitting the Ground Running
Diane Galpin, Jenny Bigmore and Jo Parker
ISBN 978 1 84905 158 3
eISBN 978 0 85700 557 1

A Practical Guide to the Mental Capacity Act 2005
Principles in Practice
Matthew Graham and Jacqueline Cowley
Foreword by Alex Ruck Keene
ISBN 978 1 84905 520 8
eISBN 978 0 85700 940 1

The Equality Act 2010 in Mental Health
A Guide to Implementation and Issues for Practice
Edited by Hári Sewell
ISBN 978 1 84905 284 9
eISBN 978 0 85700 589 2

Improving Mental Health through Social Support
Building Positive and Empowering Relationships
Jonathan Leach
ISBN 978 1 84905 518 5
eISBN 978 0 85700 932 6

Promoting Public Mental Health and Well-being
Principles into Practice
Jean S. Brown, Alyson M. Learmonth and Catherine J. Mackereth
Foreword by John Ashton
ISBN 978 1 84905 567 3
eISBN 978 1 78450 004 7

A Multidisciplinary Handbook of Child and Adolescent Mental Health for Front-line Professionals
2nd Edition
Nisha Dogra, Andrew Parkin, Fiona Gale and Clay Frake
ISBN 978 1 84310 644 9
eISBN 978 1 84642 846 3

Safeguarding Adults and the Law
2nd Edition
Michael Mandelstam
ISBN 978 1 84905 300 6
eISBN 978 0 85700 626 4

CONTENTS

FOREWORD

If we consider the range of mental disorders, from autism in childhood to schizophrenia in adults to dementia in old age, then it is estimated that at least one in five people will suffer a mental disorder at some point in their lives. Of the many varieties of mental disorders which affect adults, some exact a more severe toll on the lives of the patient and their families. Schizophrenia, bipolar disorder and major depressive disorders clearly stand out among these conditions not least because they have their onset in youth, prior to which time the person was often functioning relatively well. They affect a person at precisely that stage when some of the key foundations of life are being laid down, from completing education to finding employment to engaging in a stable relationship. No wonder then that these three are among the leading mental disorders in the global burden of disease league table. Equally importantly, those who are affected by these disorders can be helped through a judicious combination of medicines, psychological treatments and social interventions.

We need no longer be nihilistic about the prognosis of people with mental disorders and it is with this positive outlook that Introducing Mental Health has been written. Apart from these three conditions, the book also deals with personality disorders (arguably the most difficult mental health problem to work with) and challenging behaviour, a subject increasingly relevant to today's frontline mental health workers. The content covers the aetiology and clinical management of these diverse conditions, taking a balanced and sensible approach to the evidence and its implications for service users and community mental health workers.

This second edition of *Introducing Mental Health* has undergone significant revisions to reflect some of the practical and paradigmatic shifts that have taken place in the nine years since it was first published. Most notably, it addresses the fact that many severely unwell and disabled people, including those who might previously have been deemed high risk or dangerous toward themselves or others, are now being supported by community care providers and unqualified, non-formally trained workers. This is reflected in the radically updated chapter on risk assessment and management. And in light of the increasingly important (yet often inappropriate) role of police and prison officers in dealing with acutely unwell people, there is a new chapter on the role of the criminal justice system in mental health care, and an updated section on legislation to reflect key changes in the Mental Health and Mental Capacity Acts. The book also addresses the growing distance between a contentious psychiatric classification which relies on diagnosis through rigid rules applied to people's psychological experiences followed by a biomedical prescription and the day to day trials and tribulations experienced by people affected by mental disorders and those seeking to support them in the journey to recovery.

This book is primarily designed for a specific audience: those who are working in a caring capacity with people with severe or chronic mental health problems. The audience may include a wide range of professionals, from nurses on a general medical ward to supported housing workers, from social workers to placement workers helping people get back to work. However, the authors have done such an admirable job in stripping off the jargon surrounding mental disorders I imagine the book may be valuable not only for professionals but for persons with mental disorders and their families as well. What is remarkable about their effort is the authors' ability to make difficult, complex subjects 'readable'. It is not an easy task to bring a light touch to a book about mental disorder while maintaining the highest standard of ethics and political correctness. The style and layout is also innovative: they have liberally used handouts and summaries, the perfect tools for trainers, and so appropriate for our growing appetite for bite-sized information.

Caroline and Connor Kinsella's labour of love, surely borne out of many years of gestation, is a perfect example of how health matters can be explained in language that is clear and straightforward without in any way diminishing the scientific basis of the material. Although their book may be aimed mainly at a Western and particularly UK-based audience, the content reflects the reality where a growing demand for mental health care is unlikely to be met by the available mental health specialists, leading to an increasingly important role for non-specialist workers – a strategy referred to as 'task-sharing' in the global health discourse. Additionally, their practical approach toward addressing the problems faced by people affected by mental disorders is similar to the person-centred approach adopted by global mental health practitioners in low-resource settings. In this sense, this book is an important new resource for global mental health practitioners in all countries.

Vikram Patel, FMedSci
London School of Hygiene and Tropical Medicine,
the Public Health Foundation of India and Sangath, India.

INTRODUCTION

A NOTE FROM THE AUTHORS

We were very proud of the first edition of *Introducing Mental Health*. Published in 2006, 'IMH' (as we came to call it) was written as a direct response to the needs of a growing group of front-line support workers delivering services in the community with relatively little training or supervision. Our purpose was very clear: to use our many years' experience in both training and hands-on practice to provide workers with a jargon-free, accessible and, above all, clear guide to working with mentally disordered people.

As trainers and practitioners we've had the pleasure of meeting people all over the UK (and beyond) who've either read the book from cover to cover or just dipped into certain chapters for advice. The best possible praise has come from those who have kept a copy of the book on an office shelf for reference when thinking about care plans or risk assessments. Others have told us how useful it has been as a reference or *aide-mémoire* when coming across particular mental health issues.

This is exactly why we wrote it! We also seem to have struck a chord with students of nursing, social work, occupational therapy and community mental health work. To hear there is many a well-thumbed and dog-eared copy in university libraries around the world makes the very late nights and silly o'clock writing sessions seem very worthwhile indeed.

But the mental health landscape has changed dramatically in the last decade. Both in-patient beds and resources generally have been drastically reduced. Mental health professionals and acute units often provide services for only the most severely ill patients, leaving charities, housing and other social care services working with individuals who present issues and have needs much greater than they envisaged when *IMH1* was first on the bookshelves.

On a brighter note, science has of course brought a new wealth of understanding to how mental illness occurs, and how it can be treated. In some cases, treatment is a misnomer. We talk about 'recovery' and helping people live with their mental health issues rather than fighting them or trying to cure what isn't necessarily curable. The explosion of social media has allowed those who were once called 'sufferers' or 'patients' to become writers, observers and commentators on their experiences. Passive has become active. We're learning how some people diagnosed with a psychiatric disorder see that disorder not as a problem or issue, but as part of who they are.

But for most of us affected by mental illness there are still major obstacles to living what most would call a happy, normal life; and in *IMH1* we tried to bring together the latest insights from the worlds of both biology and society to try and both explain mental illness, and outline how the latest advances can help us support service users.

Much of what was current in 2006 has of course been superseded. The human genome is now available to download from your nearest web browser, and cutting-edge science in the shape of genetic studies and sophisticated scanning have given us insights into the biology of mental health only imagined nine years ago.

But as the physiology of mental illness becomes increasingly important as a means of explaining mental disorders such as depression, social and psychological approaches to assessment, treatment and recovery have also increased in importance. The global mental health movement is leading the way in finding practical, positive and, above all, effective means of support for those in developing countries with little or no access to trained professionals (Patel 2003; van Ginneken *et al.* 2013). In the UK, services once provided by NHS Trusts and mental health professionals are become increasingly scarce, while charities, housing support providers and social care agencies are taking up some of the roles once purely provided by medical psychiatry, with treatment options often limited to medication and the occasional in-patient admission.

Now, as then, we hope this new edition of *Introducing Mental Health* will become a valuable reference point for those services now providing an increasingly large proportion of mental health care. And when we say 'services' we no longer mean solely the health and social services professionals, nor the supported housing and community support providers. We include the uniformed professionals playing an ever-growing role in mental health care. The prison officers working with some of the most unwell and vulnerable individuals. The police men and women often filling in for the mental health professionals who used to provide crisis intervention and mental health assessments in the community. And of course the staff of the emergency departments seeing a growing number of people who have harmed themselves, can't cope or simply have nowhere else to go.

Divided into subject headings that focus on areas particularly relevant to those groups outlined above, this second edition contains clear outlines of some of the major issues and situations workers will encounter, together with key principles and simple techniques that can be used to help a wide variety of clients who at times present us with complex and problematic scenarios. We have also tried to make sense of the most frequently encountered psychiatric terminologies (in other words, the 'jargon') and explode some of the many myths that abound in this field.

With literally dozens of different diagnoses and a highly complicated arrangement of symptoms, behaviours and personality traits that staff will come across on a daily basis, we have drawn on our extensive experience from the worlds of both training and hands-on practice to produce an accessible, jargon-free book that focuses attention on the people and situations most likely to be encountered in day-to-day mental health care.

Using this book

Readers will be aware of the range of terms used to describe the recipients of our services. 'Tenants', 'residents', 'patients', 'clients' or 'service users' are all in common use, but we have limited our terminology to 'service users' and 'patients' as and when necessary.

Each chapter looks at a particular area of interest and is divided into sections that define terms, outline key concepts and offer key skills and techniques to help readers address some of the most common problems encountered in day-to-day work.

The 'Infoboxes' offer further explanatory notes to complement the main text, while the 'Casenotes' sections offer realistic descriptions of people and situations to help readers apply the factual material to familiar scenarios in the real world. Further reading and research can be carried out with the help of the references and resources lists provided at the end of each chapter. We have tried to select references that, as much as possible, were easily and in most cases freely available online at the time of writing and that will offer readers a much more detailed view of the subject matter.

And finally, with a vast body of further reading and research available both online and off, we provide pointers to some of the best books, blogs and other social media resources out there that will enhance and enrich the subjects we've covered here.

References

Patel, V. (2003) *Where There Is No Psychiatrist: A Mental Health Care Manual.* London: Royal College of Psychiatry Publications.

van Ginneken, N., Tharyan, P., Lewin, S., Rao, G.N. *et al.* (2013, 19 November) 'Non-specialist health worker interventions for the care of mental, neurological and substance-abuse disorders in low- and middle-income countries.' *Cochrane Database of Systematic Reviews 11*, CD009149.

Chapter 1

SEVERE AND ENDURING MENTAL ILLNESS

Mental illness continues to be one of the most misunderstood, mythologised and controversial of issues. Described for as long as human beings have been able to record thoughts and behaviours, it is at once a medical, social and at times political issue. It can lead to detention against one's will and has its very own Act of Parliament, and yet we really know very little about it.

Societies through the ages have responded to this mystery by the locking up of people whose sometimes bizarre behaviour was deemed dangerous, unsuitable or just plain scandalous. Only within the relatively recent past have the tall, thick walls of the asylum been dismantled and those who remained institutionalised and hidden allowed out into the community.

Little wonder then that mental health and mental disorder remain misunderstood to most, and frightening to many. Recent reports suggest that stigma is on the decline (Time to Change 2014) but progress has been slow. Despite the best efforts of soap scriptwriters, high-profile celebrities 'coming clean' about mental illness, and the work of mental health charities and support groups in demystifying diagnoses such as depression, we still see and hear many examples of discrimination and myth.

Given the sheer ubiquity of mental illness throughout the world, the stigma and mystery is surprising. The most recent national survey confirms the now well-known statistic that just under one in four English adults are experiencing a diagnosable mental disorder at any one time (McManus *et al.* 2009). Depression is identified by the World Health Organization as the world's leading cause of years of life lost due to disability (WHO 2009).

Relatively few of those experiencing mental health problems will come to the attention of a GP, let alone a mental health professional. This is especially so in the developing world where initiatives to develop local mental health interventions are gaining considerable ground after generations of cultural stigma and ignorance (WHO 2009). But even in parts of the world where people have ready access to medical help, many suffer alone rather than face the apparent shame of experiencing mental health problems.

Perhaps part of our reluctance to accept mental illness lies with difficulties determining mental *health*. We are made aware of factors that determine positive mental health. Connecting with people, being active, learning new things, acts of altruism and being aware of oneself (NHS 2014) have been evidenced as ways of promoting our well-being, but mental order remains rather more loosely defined than mental *disorder*.

Defining mental illness

So what are the systems used to categorise and define mental illness? In the United Kingdom, mental health professionals often refer to an ICD-10 diagnosis to refer to a patient's condition. This is the World Health Organization's (WHO) diagnostic manual, which lists all recognised (by WHO at least) diseases and disorders, including the category 'mental and behavioural disorders' (WHO 1992). The *Diagnostic and Statistical Manual of Mental Disorders* (better known as DSM-5) is more often used in the United States and elsewhere in the world (American Psychiatric Association 2013). These two sets of standards are intended to provide global standards for the recognition of mental health problems for both day-to-day clinical practice and clinical researchers, although the tools used by the latter group to measure symptoms often vary from place to place and can interfere with the 'validity' of results, or in other words the ability of one set of results to be compared with those from a different research team.

ICD-10 'mental and behavioural disorders' lists 99 different types of mental health problem, each of which is further sub-divided into a variety of more precise diagnoses, ranging from the relatively common and well known (such as depression or schizophrenia) to more obscure diagnoses such as 'specific developmental disorders of scholastic skills'.

The idea of using classification systems and labels to describe the highly complex vagaries of the human mind often meets with fierce resistance in mental health circles. The 'medical model' of psychiatry – diagnosis, prognosis and treatment – is essentially a means of applying the same scientific principles to the study and treatment of the mind as physical medicine applies to diseases of the body. An X-ray of the mind is impossible, a blood test will reveal nothing about how a person feels, and fitting a collection of psychiatric symptoms into a precise diagnostic category does not always yield a consistent result.

In psychiatry, symptoms often overlap with one another. For example, a person with obsessive compulsive disorder may believe that if they do not switch the lights on and off a certain number of times and in a particular order then a disaster will befall them. To most, this would appear a bizarre belief, to the extent that the inexperienced practitioner may label that person as 'delusional' or 'psychotic'. Similarly, a person in the early stages of Alzheimer's disease may often experience many of the 'textbook' features of clinical depression, such as low mood, poor motivation and disturbed sleep. In fact, given the tragic and predictable consequences of dementia it is unsurprising that sufferers often require treatment for depression, particularly while they retain the awareness to know that they are suffering from a degenerative condition with little or no improvement likely.

Psychiatry may often be a less-than-precise science, but the various diagnostic terms are commonplace in health and social care and have at least some descriptive power, although it is also important to remember that patients or clients may experience a complex array of feelings, experiences or 'symptoms' that may vary widely with the individual over time and from situation to situation.

Infobox: Illness or disorder?

Mental health problems can be seen as a continuum varying from normal reactions to everyday events, to serious disability requiring long-term support. The terms 'mental 'illness' or mental 'disorder' are often used interchangeably, but is there a difference?

Mental 'illness' is considered to have a clearly defined and recognisable onset after a period of 'normal functioning'. This is usually taken to mean a condition that begins to manifest later in life after a relatively healthy childhood, although adolescents and even children do suffer from mental illness. The meaning of 'illness' in this context might also be thought of as a condition having an organic or biological basis that responds to medications designed to redress imbalances of chemicals, such as the neurotransmitters described on page 25. Mental health professionals usually think of mental illness as a severe and potentially debilitating condition, such as schizophrenia or bipolar disorder, although someone suffering from severe depression might also be considered 'mentally ill'.

On the other hand, mental 'disorder' is a persistent but usually less debilitating condition that has at least some basis in childhood development. Typically, a disorder may be treated with medication, although psychological treatments such as counselling or group therapy are usually considered to be of at least equal importance in addressing the patient's problems. Examples of a mental disorder might include personality disorder, anxiety, obsessive compulsive disorder or less severe forms of depression.

A matter of degrees

Defining what is (or what is not) a mental health problem is really a matter of degrees. Nobody could be described as having 'good' mental health every minute of every day. Any football supporter will report the highs and lows encountered on an average Saturday afternoon, and can easily remember the euphoria of an important win or the despondency felt when their team is thrashed six-nil on a cold, wet Tuesday evening. But this could hardly be described as a 'mental health problem', and for all but the most ardent supporters their mood will have lifted within a short space of time.

However, the same person faced with redundancy, illness or the loss of a close family member might encounter something more akin to a 'problem'. They may experience, for example, anger, low mood, tearfulness, sleep difficulties and loss of appetite. This is a quite normal reaction to stressful life events, although the nature and degree of reaction is of course dependent on a number of factors, such as the individual's personality, the circumstances of the loss and the support available from those around them at the time. In most circumstances the bereaved person will recover after a period of time and will return to a normal way of life without the need for medical intervention of any kind. On the other hand, many people will experience mental health problems serious enough to warrant a visit to their GP.

The majority of people with mental health problems are successfully assessed and treated by GPs and other primary care professionals, such as counsellors. The Improving Access to Psychological Therapies (IAPT) programme is a now well-established approach to treating mental health problems in the community. GPs can make an IAPT referral for depressed and/or anxious patients who have debilitating mental health issues but who don't require more specialised input from a psychiatrist or community mental health nurse. Most people receiving help for psychological problems will normally be able to carry on a reasonably normal lifestyle either during treatment or following a period of recovery. A small proportion of more severe mental health issues will necessitate referral to a Community Mental Health Team (CMHT), with a smaller still group of patients needing in-patient admission or detention under the Mental Health Act.

Mental health is a continuum at the far end of which lies what professionals refer to as severe and enduring mental illness. This is a poorly defined category, but can be said to include those who suffer from severely debilitating disorders that drastically reduce their quality of life and that may necessitate long-term support from family, carers, community care providers, supported housing agencies and charities. The severe and enduring mentally ill will usually have diagnoses of severe depression or psychotic illness, and will in most cases have some degree of contact with mental health professionals.

This chapter aims to identify and describe the most well-known and debilitating mental illnesses, and to clear up some of the misunderstanding that surrounds terms such as psychosis, schizophrenia, bipolar disorder and depression.

What is psychosis?

The word 'psychosis' originates from the Greek words *psyche* meaning 'mind' and *osis* meaning 'condition'. It is not a diagnosis in itself but a collective term for diagnoses such as schizophrenia and bipolar disorder, and describes a collection of symptoms that usually renders the sufferer unable to maintain anything like a normal lifestyle.

It is a term thoroughly enjoyed by writers of tabloid headlines, usually as part of some gruesome story of serial killers or extreme violence. But psychosis means a great deal more than this, and certainly doesn't describe inevitable murder or catastrophe.

A psychotic person is someone who, to a greater or lesser extent, has lost touch with the real world, often to the extent that they hold false and sometimes troubling beliefs, or experience sounds, sights or even smells that only they can detect. For example, the person might believe that their neighbours are attempting to poison them, or that they have special powers bestowed upon them by the internet. They may hear voices telling them to act in certain ways, or describing them as dirty or evil. In severe circumstances the psychotic person may speak in riddles, or with jumbled words and sentences that make sense to them but not to anyone else, and may behave strangely or even, at times, dangerously. In most cases, psychosis is easily detectable to everyone except the sufferer him or herself. In other words, the sufferer has no insight into their beliefs, experiences and behaviours, which appear to them entirely normal.

Psychosis is a broad term encompassing a number of symptoms and several diagnoses, which typically include schizophrenia, bipolar disorder and a number of other conditions, such as depression and dementia. But diagnosis in mental health has for decades been a subjective and at times controversial topic, and recent science has begun to suggest major changes in the way we think about psychosis and severe mental illness.

The problem of diagnosis

A significant body of genetic and biological evidence has begun to point to difficulty with the current classification of psychotic mental illnesses as discrete standalone concepts. Schizophrenia, bipolar disorder and most of the other mental disorders have always proved elusive to researchers looking for the 'smoking gun' that determines a person's genetic vulnerability to becoming mentally ill. But huge technological advances have allowed researchers to take a more wide-angle approach to the whole human genome. What they have found so far poses a major challenge to the traditional classifications of abnormal mental health as distinct disease entities, and may even require an entire overhaul of the world's two psychiatric classification systems.

Genetically speaking, there appears little to distinguish between familiar diagnoses such as bipolar disorder and schizophrenia (Craddock and Owen 2010). There also appears to be a significant genetic overlap between schizophrenia and other major diagnoses, such as autism and depression (Smoller *et al.* 2013). Clusters of slight genetic abnormality have been identified up and down the human genome that accurately predict certain phenomena, such as delusional ideas or hallucinations, but are not associated with our traditional diagnostic models. In short, what has been recognised for more than a century as schizophrenia or depression or bipolar disorder may come to be better described as a 'psychotic disorder' or 'mood disorder', with symptoms that are fairly typical to those terms but not exclusively so.

This will come as little surprise to those who have long been far from convinced as to the accuracy and reliability of psychiatric diagnosis. Depressed people often experience feelings of paranoia. People diagnosed as schizophrenic may experience periods of intense mania, or sadness, something that has traditionally been associated with bipolar disorder.

And while we have long known that bipolar disorder and schizophrenia can run in families, it is striking that the child of mentally ill parents may well develop mental illness as an adult, but not necessarily the same illness. In short, it seems increasingly likely that the future of professional psychiatry rests on a focused formulation of a patient's thoughts, feelings, behaviour and social situation rather than the identification of a standardised label that attempts to collect signs and symptoms into a simple diagnostic 'box'.

If this poses a certain difficulty to writers of textbooks such as this, it will hopefully lead to more sophisticated approaches to severe mental illness. A clearer picture of the genetic abnormalities leading to each individual's profile of problems and symptoms may lead the way to focused psychological and pharmaceutical treatments based on the patient, not the disease.

Such paradigm shifts are, for now, sure to be some years away, and we will stay with the more familiar terminologies for the remainder of this book.

Neurotransmitters

Serotonin

There are theories that serotonin is involved in everything from falling in love (Marazziti *et al.* 1999) to an increased risk of suicide, an association that has become increasingly controversial given the widespread prescribing of anti-depressants, which increase levels of serotonin (Ferguson *et al.* 2005; Reid and Barbui 2010).

Surprisingly, most of the body's stock of serotonin is to be found in the gastro-intestinal tract rather than the brain. Although often known as a 'mood hormone' and the chemical most directly involved in the effects of Ecstasy and other recreational drugs, serotonin is closely related to several forms of animal venom and performs an essential role in regulating the circulatory system.

Serotonin is closely related to sleep regulation, memory and learning as well as being largely responsible for triggering peristalsis (the passage of food through the gut). It has been known for some time that the nerve cells of depressed people have a tendency to metabolise serotonin too efficiently, leaving the brain with abnormally low levels. Modern anti-depressants (the selective serotonin reuptake inhibitors or SSRIs) block off these receptors, making more serotonin available to the brain and thus improving mood.

Noradrenaline

Noradrenaline is chemically very similar to the adrenaline most people know from the familiar 'fright, fight or flight syndrome' learnt in school biology lessons. Although noradrenaline is a vasoconstrictor (narrowing the diameter of blood vessels) and is sometimes used to treat shock and low blood pressure in emergency situations, as a nervous system neurotransmitter it has also been found to have a similar role to seratonin in regulating mood, and is associated with the psychological processes such as motivation and reward. As with seratonin, low levels of noradrenaline are associated with depression. The pathways and mechanisms of both neurotransmitters overlap with one another, and several of the newer anti-depressants target both seratonin and noradrenaline receptors.

Dopamine

Dopamine is an interesting neurotransmitter closely associated with both of the above. Dopamine is one of the key agents involved in co-ordination and movement. The symptoms of the movement disorder Parkinson's disease are caused by the brain's inability to produce sufficient quantities of dopamine, resulting in poor communication between the brain and the muscular system. Dopamine has an important psychological role in the experience of pleasure, and recreational drugs such as amphetamines and cocaine act on dopamine receptors, making more dopamine available to the brain. It is also closely associated with cognitive processes such as memory, attention and problem solving, and is believed to play an important role in the mind's association between stimuli and reward. Recent theories suggest that dopamine influences our tendency to look forward to experiences we know to be pleasurable, as well as highlighting potentially threatening or dangerous things.

Dopamine overactivity is well known to be associated with the symptoms of psychosis. Anti-psychotic drugs work by blocking dopamine receptors. However, older types of anti-psychotics tended to be somewhat over-zealous in this respect, sometimes resulting in side-effects that resembled the tremor and other symptoms of Parkinson's disease. Newer 'atypical' anti-psychotics are more selective in their blocking action, less sedating and target a wider range of symptoms than their predecessors.

Glutamate

Glutamate is a surprisingly familiar neurotransmitter, especially if we enjoy Chinese food or Marmite on toast. Monosodium glutamate as a food additive was discovered by boiling seaweed, and is now made in vast quantities by fermenting wheat.

Glutamate is actually an amino acid (the building blocks of protein) present in quite large quantities in our brains, but only recently revealed as a possible major component in the development of psychosis. Much research has been focused on a lack of glutamate interacting with over-production of dopamine in people with schizophrenia (Moghaddam and Javitt 2012).

Schizophrenia

This is a widely misunderstood term commonly referred to as meaning 'split personality'. 'Schizophrenic' is increasingly and quite wrongly used by the media as an adjective to indicate a dichotomy, or a division into two. Journalists refer to a 'schizophrenic government'. Weather forecasters might describe weather as 'a bit schizophrenic'. Schizophrenia doesn't confer any 'Jekyll and Hyde' characteristics but does have profound effects on how the sufferer thinks, feels and behaves. It is an illness that can profoundly affect the personality, but certainly doesn't 'split' it.

Prevalence

Between 0.3 and 0.7 per cent of people will develop schizophrenia at some stage during their lives (Van Os and Kapur 2009). These figures are, however, sensitive to how diagnosis is defined, and vary widely according to geography and social demographic factors. Differences in incidence of schizophrenia between rural and city dwellers have been apparent both to researchers and those of us who work in community mental health (Häfner 2014). Nonetheless, schizophrenia is a condition that exists in every part of the world and in all ethnic groups, and has been described to varying degrees of accuracy for several thousand years.

The severity and level of lifelong disability varies considerably. Just under half of all newly diagnosed people will experience a good outcome with few if any long-term effects (Menezes, Arenovich and Zipursky 2006). Some will have occasional recurrences with limited impact on quality of life, but for others schizophrenia represents a lifelong condition that will have serious effects on their ability to lead what most of us would call a 'normal' life. It is this group who are most likely to come into contact with the readership of this book.

What causes schizophrenia?

Recent evidence points toward schizophrenia as a biological condition strongly influenced by early childhood and developmental factors (Häfner 2014). We are used to thinking of schizophrenia as an illness that tends to wait for adolescence or early adulthood before erupting into full-blown disorder. The 'neurodevelopmental' explanation suggests a condition more akin to autism, with certain clues and early indicators present from a very early age. Most people now diagnosed with schizophrenia will recall a childhood free of dramatic phenomena such as hallucinations, delusions and thought disorder, but family members may describe a child who was socially withdrawn or 'a little odd'. Researchers have identified cognitive and educational deficits among children who go on to develop schizophrenia. Mental health professionals describe these as 'prodromal' or 'warning signs', which will typically develop and intensify as the individual approaches full-blown or 'florid' mental illness in early adulthood. Life event stress, such as bereavement or starting university, seem to be common trigger factors for the more obvious and debilitating manifestations of schizophrenia. The combination of brain chemistry, genetic vulnerability and the environment is a process that seems important to describing the cause(s) of schizophrenia.

Schizophrenia has long been known as having an inherited component. There is certainly little doubt that schizophrenia along with other psychotic disorders, such as bipolar disorder, are hereditary to some degree. In fact, a diagnosis of schizophrenia or bipolar disorder is much more common in descendants of people with either of the above diagnoses, a fact that has both clouded research efforts and led to the evidence that schizophrenia and bipolar disorder are perhaps better described as points along a continuum of psychotic illness than two distinct diagnoses in their own right (Craddock and Owen 2010).

Some of the causal factors associated with schizophrenia can be surprising. Being born in the winter, having a mother who suffered flu during pregnancy, premature birth and oxygen starvation at birth have all been found to have a stronger than chance association with a later diagnosis of schizophrenia (McGrath *et al.* 2008).

Immigrant status has long been associated with schizophrenia. Long before the still troubling observation that black people were far more likely to be diagnosed with severe mental illness than their white neighbours in countries such as the US and UK, Norwegian immigrants to Minnesota in the early 20th century were observed to be twice as likely to be admitted to hospital for schizophrenia as Norwegians who had stayed in their country of birth (Odegaard 1932). Subsequent studies have further demolished any idea of schizophrenia as a racial or ethnic weakness (Häfner 2014).

Mental health workers will be familiar with particularly heavy use of both cannabis and nicotine by the severely mentally ill, but more recent evidence has suggested that a predisposition to begin smoking cannabis is actually associated with a higher risk of developing schizophrenia (Power *et al.* 2014). There can be little doubt that heavy cannabis use in adolescence contributes to an elevated risk of psychotic illness in later life (Casadio *et al.* 2011), but claims that the drug actually causes schizophrenia are far from accurate.

So, now we know some of the key environmental factors that can predict a higher risk of schizophrenia. But more recent science has begun to take a very detailed look at the genetic factors that could only be glimpsed until a few years ago.

Genetic studies combined with advanced scanning techniques lead toward a theory of a brain that is particularly vulnerable to schizophrenia in later life, but that also has similarities to the brains of people on the autistic spectrum. It is now well known that schizophrenia is associated with both chemical and structural brain dysfunction. Anti-psychotic medication works on blocking pathways for brain chemicals such as dopamine and serotonin. Another neurotransmitter called glutamate is currently the target of much research into the pathways involved in schizophrenia and its effects (Moghaddam and Javitt 2012). The emergent complexity of the brain pathology involved with schizophrenia points toward pharmaceutical solutions that can, for the time being, offer little more than a 'one size fits all' option, which successfully counters some, but by no means all of the negative effects of psychotic illness, and which have little if any benefit for some individuals.

While genetic factors are an undoubtedly important area of further research into the causes of schizophrenia, the role of heredity does not offer a simple cause-and-effect relationship, and our knowledge in this area has been complicated both by problems of definition (of schizophrenia) and by 'confounding factors' such as the environment in which a child has been brought up. Not all 'high-risk' children develop schizophrenia in adulthood, and some develop the illness with no family history whatsoever, but recent advances in relating individual genes to specific brain abnormalities are leading the way toward a more subtle and much greater understanding of how a person develops schizophrenia (Owen, O'Donovan and Harrison 2005).

So to sum up, there is no neat and tidy way of explaining why someone with schizophrenia came to be diagnosed with this potentially devastating illness. We know now that are certain weaknesses and anomalies along the genome of the affected individual, which are inherited from one or both parents and predict a certain vulnerability to schizophrenia and, as now seems likely, other serious mental illnesses as well (Smoller *et al.* 2013).

This genetic picture quite possibly interacts with factors in the person's environment (both pre- and post-birth) to create abnormalities in brain structure and chemical function. These in turn lead to possible cognitive and social functioning deficits as the child develops, and impairments in how an individual processes and interprets information. Combined with exposure to trigger factors, such as stress in adolescence and early adulthood, or heavy use of drugs or alcohol, full-blown emergence of hallucinations, thought disorder and delusions may be the end result of a process that has been developing since conception.

Consequences of schizophrenia

Schizophrenia is a potentially severe and debilitating illness if not diagnosed and treated as quickly as possible. Early intervention by mental health professionals dramatically reduces the risk of the illness becoming a major long-term disability, but people with schizophrenia usually have more difficulty than most forming and maintaining relationships. People with schizophrenia seldom have a wide network of friends and acquaintances prior to symptoms emerging, and may have been previously described by parents and teachers as isolated and withdrawn compared with their peers. Social withdrawal is often accentuated in the early stages of schizophrenia, with families often concerned that their son or daughter has locked themselves away in a bedroom, becoming disconnected from the outside world and behaving oddly. Once the illness has fully emerged in adulthood the sufferer may also have difficulty working, and generally going about the day-to-day aspects of life most of us take for granted, such as driving a car or renting a flat. Schizophrenia often demands high levels of support and social care from families, mental health professionals and social care agencies.

One particularly alarming statistic associated with schizophrenia is greatly reduced life expectancy. Sufferers die on average 10 to 25 years earlier than usual (Laursen *et al.* 2013). Early death may be well known to mental professionals as an inevitable consequence of poverty, poor housing, heavy smoking and substance misuse associated with schizophrenia. People with schizophrenia are also more likely to commit suicide than the general population (Hor and Taylor 2010). But more recent work points to inherent metabolic and cardiovascular issues associated with the diagnosis, and is leading to growing awareness and intervention with projects such as Healthy Active Lives (HeAL) (Shiers and Curtis 2014), which aim to enhance early intervention in psychosis services with much greater emphasis on physical screening and long-term health.

We have already highlighted a strong association between substance misuse and psychotic illness. Mental health workers sometimes refer to 'dual diagnosis' as a combination of a severe mental illness with a substance misuse disorder, but this definition fails to differentiate between 'use' and 'abuse' and is now so prevalent an issue that its standing as a standalone phenomenon appears limited. Heavy use/abuse of drugs and alcohol seems endemic among the severely mentally ill. Figures vary widely, but alcohol and cannabis in particular are very heavily used by people with psychotic illnesses, including schizophrenia. There are subsequent associations between drugs, alcohol and other potential consequences, such as the risk of violence or suicide, increased rates of poor physical health, reduced adherence with treatment and support and suicide.

Symptoms of schizophrenia

The symptoms of schizophrenia are identified as belonging to one of two groups: positive or negative. Positive symptoms, such as thought disorder, delusions, hallucinations and loss of insight, are more immediately obvious and are those features that are most likely to be identified by families, friends or teachers as an indication that all is not well. In the longer term, negative symptoms, such as apathy, social withdrawal and lack of energy, may become more apparent. It is these effects along with cognitive impairment that appear to have a more profound effect on overall quality of life than the voices, delusions and paranoid ideas that most people immediately associate with this condition.

THOUGHT DISORDER

Thought disorder is a key indicator of schizophrenia, and can take the form of 'thought blocking' (not being able to think logically), 'thought insertion' (believing someone is putting thoughts into one's head) and 'thought broadcasting' (believing other people can hear one's thoughts).

The sufferer is unable to think in a logical progression, and thoughts and ideas may be heavily influenced and further confused by delusional ideas and hallucinations as described below. To the outside world this is most likely to become evident in a person's pattern of speech, which becomes erratic and confused. A thought-disordered person's conversation appears jumbled as the individual jumps from topic to topic with little or no coherent pattern. Communication with the sufferer may become difficult if not impossible. Skilled and experienced mental health workers will know that simplicity is the key, and will attempt a very narrow focus of conversation in order to maintain at least some communication and rapport with the thought-disordered person.

DELUSIONS

Another indicator of schizophrenia is the presence of delusions. These are beliefs that are bizarre, at odds with a person's cultural experience, and unable to be proved objectively to be true. The person may describe being watched, for example by hidden cameras or microphones. They may believe that the television or radio is communicating directly with them, or that their thoughts are being broadcast to others and are no longer private.

Medical reports may refer to 'passivity phenomena' or 'control experiences', meaning that the sufferer feels their thoughts and actions are controlled by a third-party, such as a real or imaginary character in that person's life, or by aliens, the church, the internet or a political party.

HALLUCINATIONS

A further diagnostic indicator looked for by psychiatrists is the presence of hallucinations. A hallucination is a sensory perception that appears real only to the person experiencing that stimulus and can involve any of the senses. People suffering from epilepsy or brain injury sometimes experience olfactory (to do with the sense of smell) or visual hallucinations, but the most frequently described experiences in schizophrenia are the auditory hallucinations or 'voices' heard by them but inaudible to anyone else. Experiences such as these are sometimes associated with other illnesses and disorders, and are sometimes described by otherwise 'normal' people who have occasionally been misdiagnosed and treated on the basis of their voices. The term 'hallucination' may prove something of a misnomer, as evidence from brain scanning studies suggests that the voices are in fact the sort of very real 'inner speech' familiar to any of us rehearsing for an interview or preparing for a meeting. In fact, parts of the brain active when we have these conversations with ourselves are also very active when people experiencing hallucinations are monitored in a brain scanner (Allen *et al.* 2007).

A person with schizophrenia may, for example, hear the voice of one or more people giving them instructions, insulting them or even telling jokes. The so-called 'command hallucinations' are, as the name suggests, voices that direct the individual to carry out certain tasks or react in a particular way. For example, a sufferer's voices may command them to carry out seemingly bizarre rituals, or to keep the presence and identity of the voices secret, or even to harm themselves or others. This sometimes creates conflict in the mind of the person experiencing the commands and appears to those around them as a bizarre and heated argument with 'themselves'. The hearing of voices is frequently described as among the most upsetting and disorientating of symptoms, particularly when sufferers are forced to resist commands that they know are destructive or anti-social, or that those around them are unable to comprehend.

LOSS OF INSIGHT

As with other forms of psychotic illness, people diagnosed with schizophrenia usually lose insight into their situation. In other words, they have little or no conception of being unwell. While mental health professionals, families and carers may clearly see a deterioration in a person's functioning and general well-being, sufferers themselves are oblivious to their situation and may take great exception to assessments, interviews and the attentions of mental health professionals. Loss of insight is a particularly disturbing aspect of schizophrenia. When a person has flu, appendicitis or even depression, they are almost always aware that they are unwell. Schizophrenia severely disrupts a person's understanding and perception of the real world, and the distressing experiences of schizophrenia are all too real to the person themselves.

Negative symptoms of schizophrenia

The phenomena described above are usually acute, or in other words are quite obvious and have an immediate impact on both the individual and those around them. However, with the appropriate identification and intervention, positive symptoms can be relatively short-lived. However, schizophrenia is also characterised by another set of features known as 'negative' symptoms, which are less obvious and more insidious and often present greater challenges to carers and mental health professionals. Social withdrawal, apathy and an inability to concentrate for long periods of time are very common features of schizophrenia that often persist long after more acute, positive symptoms have disappeared.

While it is certainly true that some of the features described here may be the result of prolonged treatment with powerful anti-psychotic drugs, negative symptoms exist even in those who have remained untreated with medication. In fact, as we shall see later in this chapter, modern 'atypical' anti-psychotic drugs are relatively free of the sedative effects of the older 'typical' anti-psychotic drugs and are designed to treat both positive and negative symptoms, the latter usually proving more difficult to treat than the more evident phenomena.

Medication aside, the carer's response to apathy, social isolation and poor or non-existent self-care is typically one of trying to look beyond the disappointment of watching the social decline of patients, clients or family members even when the more distressing features of the illness have subsided. A person may remain in bed all day, or sit in front of a television, or refuse all interaction with others, or refuse to wash, shower or change their clothes for weeks at a time.

Bipolar disorder

Still sometimes known as manic depression, bipolar disorder is a severe mental illness that, like schizophrenia, belongs to the psychosis group of disorders. It affects around one in two hundred people worldwide and shares many features with schizophrenia. The fact that it tends to run in families alongside schizophrenia, responds to the same anti-psychotic drugs and shares much of the newly discovered genetic variation with other mental illnesses has cast doubt on its identity as a separate diagnosis (Craddock and Owen 2010).

Nonetheless sufferers and many mental health professionals will continue to see bipolar disorder as a distinct illness with its own identity and a quite particular profile of short- and long-term effects. Schizophrenia is often associated with long-term decline in cognitive and social abilities. The most severely affected may need support from health and social care services for most of their adult lives.

Bipolar disorder appears in most, if not all, experiences to have less damaging long-term effects. Sufferers are on the whole more likely than those diagnosed with schizophrenia to have relationships, families and careers. In other words, to be able to lead a relatively normal and independent life in between the extremes of profound low mood on the one hand, and bizarre, grandiose over-excitement on the other.

This is a mental illness with an almost romantic association with art and creativity. An online search will reveal long lists of singers, entrepreneurs, writers, actors and artists who have revealed themselves as bipolar sufferers. This link with celebrity and creativity may give some the impression that bipolar is not a severe mental illness, and for some it remains well controlled with only occasional bouts of disorder. But others will be subject to more severe bouts of disruption with only short periods of what mental health professionals refer to as 'baseline' or normal mental health. This is a group much more likely than the business people or celebrities to experience long-term, severe disability with perhaps crisis intervention from mental health services and admission to in-patient units.

We can see now that bipolar disorder is a difficult to define mental illness but is characterised for the most part by periods of normality interspersed by severe low mood or extreme excitement and overactivity. The popular view of bipolar disorder is that these two states of mania and depression alternate neatly with one another. The sufferer experiences periods of extreme elation followed by bouts of equally extreme low mood. The real picture is usually more complex than this, with one mood state being experienced more frequently and more severely than the other. As there are several variants of the illness with different patterns of low mood and overactivity, some mental health professionals refer to bipolar spectrum disorder, bipolar affective disorder ('affect' meaning 'mood') or bipolar I and bipolar II.

The fact that the severity and impact of the condition varies widely from person to person is mediated partly by brain chemistry and genetic factors, but also to a very large extent by supportive factors such as the support of family and friends, help from health and social care services, medication and the person's own knowledge and awareness of early warning signs and how to seek help.

On the other hand, the 'rapid cycling' form of bipolar disorder, where extremes of mood are experienced more than four times within a year, may leave the sufferer disabled by altered moods and psychotic symptoms for much of their adult life and cause significant lifestyle disruption. Severity of symptoms and rapid cycling have been associated with cognitive impairment (a reduced ability to think, reason and solve problems) and social disability whereby the sufferer faces great difficulties in forming and maintaining relationships, finding employment or enjoying many of the lifestyle norms most of us take for granted.

Like schizophrenia, bipolar disorder has a negative impact on physical health and mortality. Rates of cardiovascular disease, diabetes, respiratory disease and other long-term conditions are elevated by bipolar disorder, particularly with the more severely debilitating forms of the illness (Crump *et al.* 2013).

Bipolar disorder typically manifests between the late teens and mid-20s, and like schizophrenia tends to develop earlier in men than women. However, clear diagnosis may take considerable time, and it is not unusual for sufferers to describe intervals of many years between first symptoms and a diagnosis being made.

Both the 'highs' and 'lows' of bipolar disorder share many features with other 'standalone' conditions, such as schizophrenia or depression, and as we have already seen, there can be considerable variation in the way this disorder presents from one person to another. When one experiences one or other of these states at different times, sometimes separated by months or even years and not necessarily following the neat pattern usually attributed to this illness, psychiatrists need to be very clear about a diagnosis before they and other professionals would want to tell a patient they are suffering from a severe and enduring mental illness that can be controlled but not cured, and will most likely affect them for the rest of their lives.

The typical picture of an individual experiencing the alternating poles of extreme 'highs' and 'lows' is for most sufferers and researchers alike an increasingly simplistic, inaccurate description. Nonetheless, it is also reasonably descriptive and recognisable, and the next section takes a closer look at what mania and depression look like in everyday life.

Bipolar mania

We use the word 'manic' in day-to-day terms to describe someone who is restless, overactive or excited. The psychiatric condition associated with bipolar disorder can be a very different and altogether more frightening phenomenon. For anyone who has either experienced or witnessed at first hand the sheer power of full-blown mania it will come as little surprise that these episodes have the potential for truly serious repercussion. Someone who is extremely active, restless, over-talkative and filled with very grand and unrealistic notions of who they are will often come into contact with the emergency services. People who are manic may dress strangely, behave bizarrely and will quickly draw attention to themselves. Police officers may be more familiar than other professionals with local people who experience intermittent episodes of mania.

Superficially at least, the person experiencing this stage of the illness may appear elated, happy and full of energy and ideas, but either manic or depressive phases of bipolar disorder are often 'triggered' by stress or untoward life events, such as bereavement or redundancy. In fact, in some cultures mania is an expression of extreme sadness or distress as opposed to the low mood and lack of motivation more often seen in the West.

Initially the manic phase may present as little more than insomnia and restlessness. For those who have experienced manic episodes before this is often a key early warning sign (see page 49), and seeking help at this stage may prevent further progression to the complete chaos of full-blown mania.

People with experience of bipolar disorder often refer to the dilemma of entering the manic phase (Adams 2002). In early stages of mania the person remains aware of what is happening and that they are becoming unwell. However, the need to seek intervention, which will usually involve some form of tranquillising medication, is compromised by the feelings of elation and the intense creativity that accompany this phase. People with a history of bipolar disorder often enthuse about the highly pleasurable aspect of mania (Adams 2002), particularly prior to the descent into full-scale, insightless chaos. They describe feelings of intense creativity and can sometimes produce evidence of this, as can dozens of famous bipolar poets, artists and novelists throughout the last century. People who have experienced mania can recall intense feelings of pleasure and 'oneness' with others, and describe with some enthusiasm the omnipotence and greatly enhanced self-esteem, which is often at odds with their usual personality. Even with the benefit of hindsight, those with a history of bipolar disorder and manic phases in particular are often torn between the lure of a wonderful few days of elation and excitement, and the knowledge that early mania is but 'the calm before the storm', and that steps need to be taken before the situation becomes catastrophic.

As mania progresses, speech becomes rapid and increasingly disorganised, jumping from topic to topic in no particular order. Two-way conversation becomes difficult if not impossible as the person appears desperate to communicate their ideas, which by this stage are appearing faster than they can talk, leading to even more rapid speech and an increase in volume. By this time extreme restlessness may have become apparent and the individual may have lost insight into their situation, crossing the boundary between the real world and their psychotic experience of extreme power, creativity and energy. Delusional beliefs of superiority, wealth and omnipotence may have surfaced by this stage. Credit card companies are constantly dealing with situations where people with bipolar disorder have spent hundreds or even thousands of pounds on shopping sprees, cars or donations to charities while unwell.

If left untreated and unsupported by families or carers, manic people may become highly vulnerable to exploitation and are easily distracted or lured into financial scams or sexual promiscuity. Behaviour becomes increasingly bizarre, often involving uncharacteristically loud clothing, extreme restlessness (running rather than walking) and public displays that may draw the attention of police. Mania is often characterised as 'elation' and the opposite extreme of depression, although irritability and aggression are not uncommon, particularly where the person's ideas are contradicted or their extremes of behaviour are curtailed.

As with schizophrenia, delusional ideas are expressed, often involving grandiose self-images of world domination/salvation/genius/omnipotence, etc. Where insight has disappeared, attempts by carers, families or health care staff to contradict numerous and sometimes bizarre ideas and theories are unlikely to be helpful. The manic person's theory that they are 'working on a machine that will bring about world peace' may appear absurd to anyone else, but contradiction will be invariably met with disbelief, frustration and sometimes anger.

By this stage, and without medical intervention and support, which may involve hospital admission, the sufferer may not have slept for several nights and, in the absence of any interest in food or drink, may have become malnourished and dehydrated.

Fortunately, modern methods of recognition and early intervention have prevented much of the chaos and embarrassment caused by mania, although living with the consequences of wild overspending and bizarre behaviour remains one of the key problems for sufferers of bipolar disorder. Sufferers often liken the 'come down' from mania as akin to the morning after a party, having to face the consequences of a drunken night of arguing, insults and outrageous behaviour eagerly reported by friends but scarcely remembered by the protagonists themselves.

Bipolar depression

Bipolar depression occurs three times more frequently than mania and is associated with suicide and impaired function and quality of life (NICE 2014a). The onset of depression in bipolar disorder is often quite sudden and dramatic, in some cases immediately following a manic phase. There is also a tendency toward greater severity of symptoms. At its most serious, bipolar depression has the potential to leave an individual mute and immobile, unable to communicate or carry out even basic tasks such as washing, dressing or eating. In direct contrast to the grandiose ideas and apparently comedic voices heard when in an elated state, psychotic symptoms often take the much darker forms of paranoia, insult and verbal abuse when that same person is descending toward extreme low mood.

Six per cent of bipolar disorder sufferers commit suicide within 20 years of diagnosis (Nordentoft, Mortensen and Pedersen 2011). The risk of suicide is always heightened by severe depression, particularly where the person is troubled by voices or delusional ideas, which in some cases may 'command' the individual into acts of self-harm or suicide.

Treatment may again be required within a safe hospital setting. In addition to the essential support of friends and family, those experiencing the depressive phase of bipolar disorder will normally be treated with anti-depressant medication. Normally prescribed on a long-term, preventative basis, the prescription of anti-depressants in bipolar disorder is a somewhat more delicate affair as there remains the risk of 'overshooting' the person's mood back into elation.

What causes bipolar disorder?

The 'aetiology' or cause of bipolar disorder is as complicated a picture as it is with schizophrenia, with much of the evidence sharing close parallels with the latter. The latest research suggests that there is no single cause of bipolar disorder, but that several key factors interact with one another. Genetics, childhood development, life stress and brain biology all appear to have a significant role in the development of the illness (Anderson, Haddad and Scott 2012). Current knowledge suggests the emergence of a model that encompasses both 'nurture' and 'nature' explanations, or put in other words, the environmental and the biological. It appears possible, if not probable, that an individual is born with a genetic predisposition to develop bipolar disorder. However, this predisposition is not confined to a single gene but a complex combination of anomalies stretching across the entirety of a sufferer's 'genome' – the genetic map contained in every cell that defines us and every other living thing. But these inherited factors are not in themselves the cause of bipolar disorder. Rather, they create a genetic potential or vulnerability to mental illness that may only be 'switched on' by factors in that person's early and adult environment. There is strong evidence that a higher than expected number of sufferers have histories of childhood trauma and abuse (Etain *et al.* 2008).

Depression

Everyone experiences feelings of low mood and despondency at some stage in their lives, but depression can be described as an 'illness' when feelings of despair, along with an inability to carry out normal day-to-day life, becomes so prolonged and severe that medical intervention is required. Professionals often refer to this as 'clinical' depression. It may affect a person as a 'one-off' event, recur at intervals throughout a person's life, or continue to affect the sufferer as a 'chronic' illness over a period of many years. While a diagnosis is made on the basis of several key symptoms, clinical depression can vary widely in both intensity and the way that it is experienced by the individual and those around them.

As we have already seen, depression can be part of bipolar disorder, but will be more familiar to most of us as a standalone condition. It is one of the world's most debilitating conditions, responsible for more lost time and absence from work than back pain, arthritis, cancer or injury. About one in 20 people will have experienced clinical depression at some stage within the previous year, although only a relatively small proportion of sufferers will seek or receive help, particularly in developing countries (WHO 2012).

Like most other mental disorders, one individual's experience of depression may be quite different from another's. The severity exists along a continuum. At its most serious and debilitating, depression may lead to an inability to move, communicate or carry out even basic tasks such as eating and drinking.

In this instance, serious physical illness and even death are immediate potential hazards and hospital admission may prove essential as will treatment with anti-depressants or, in emergency situations, electro-convulsive therapy (ECT) (see page 72). The person will also need assistance with nutrition, hydration and basic self-care tasks.

Less severe episodes of depression are more common but may nonetheless leave the sufferer incapable of most everyday tasks and frightened of meeting others. They may be unwilling to leave the house or even get out of bed without considerable effort, and suicidal thoughts are not uncommon. Medical assessment and intervention in such cases is almost always required, with an assessment of suicide risk forming a key determinant of whether the person will require more intrusive interventions, such as hospital admission or close monitoring at home by relatives and mental health professionals.

While the scenarios outlined above represent emergency situations with high risks of harm to the individual concerned, complete recovery is possible, particularly with the benefit of ongoing drug treatments and 'talking therapies' such as those described in Chapter 2.

Alternatively depression may sometimes be experienced as an ongoing or 'chronic' condition that can nonetheless be tolerated and managed to the extent that a person is able to carry on a reasonably normal lifestyle, including work and family responsibilities. However, they may not enjoy life to the same extent as most people and may experience a negative, pessimistic outlook on life. Stress or upsetting life events may prove more difficult than for most people and may prompt more severe symptoms, such as loss of appetite, sleep disturbance or suicidal thoughts.

Whatever the severity or impact of illness on the person's life, depression sufferers cannot simply 'snap out of it'. They will need the ongoing support of family, friends and health professionals alongside appropriate drug treatments and psychological therapies. If depression is a recurring problem, onset will usually be relatively gradual and early warning signs (see page 49) can be identified to prompt immediate action that may prevent further deterioration or slow down the progress of the more debilitating symptoms.

A diagnosis of depression will usually be made on the basis of a patient's self-report, but information from a friend or relative may prove invaluable, particularly in situations where the person has difficulty expressing their feelings or is unable to communicate at all. Persistent low mood is obviously a key diagnostic factor, but other symptoms, such as sleep disturbance, loss of appetite or loss of interest in normally enjoyable activities, will often be noted along with a general feeling of hopelessness and very low self-esteem. A depressed person often experiences intrusive, negative thoughts, with constant rumination over past events, current problems or perceived disasters yet to come. They may voice beliefs such as 'What is the point of living?' or 'Everyone hates me, including me!' that will not respond to any amount of reassurance from those around them.

Tiredness and fatigue are almost always associated with depression, although it is not uncommon for people to throw themselves into work or other activities in a usually vain attempt to 'shrug off' their feelings or divert themselves from constant negative thoughts.

Substance misuse and dependence have a close relationship with depression, with heavy drinkers and drug users being more likely to be clinically depressed than the general population (Haynes *et al.* 2005). However, the relationship represents something of a 'chicken or egg' situation and it is important for mental health professionals to determine whether heavy substance use precedes depression or is an attempt by the already depressed person to mask symptoms, blot out feelings or 'self-medicate'.

As mentioned above, some individuals are unable to articulate their feelings verbally. Whether this is due to learning disability, the language barrier or the 'retardation' caused by depression itself, carers can still identify this condition by awareness of the features outlined above and discuss with a GP or mental health professional to avoid either a first episode or any deterioration of an existing depressive illness.

Many languages and cultures have no equivalent of 'depression' as it is understood in the English language. Health professionals working with ethnic minority communities will be well aware that a number of people will experience depression as 'somatic' or physical health problems such as recurrent headaches, stomach pains or flu-like symptoms (Patel 2001). A significant number of depressed GP attenders are only identified as suffering from depression through reports of physical health problems (Ahmed and Bhugra 2007).

What causes depression?

At the risk of sounding repetitive, no single cause of depression has yet been identified. The causes of depression are as complex and varied as the manifestations of the illness itself, and appear to be a combination of genetic, biological and 'life event' factors. Significant changes in brain structure have been found to be associated with forms of depression that are particularly severe and persistent (Kempton *et al.* 2011). Traumatic childhood and life events such as abuse, bereavement or physical illness play a major part in depression, as do social factors such as unemployment, relationship problems or poor housing (Kinderman 2013). First instances of depression, or relapses of an existing illness, are frequently preceded by stress, trauma, physical illness or bereavement, but the exact mechanism of how external events impact upon a person's internal world to the extent that they may be rendered suicidal, mute or incapable of looking after themselves remains elusive.

Seasonal affective disorder (SAD) is however one rare example of a psychiatric condition with a relatively simple cause-and-effect mechanism, with an equally uncomplicated treatment. In the northern hemisphere, sufferers only experience symptoms between the months of September and April each year. Seasonal affective disorder is a form of depression triggered by the comparative absence of natural light during the autumn and winter months. Natural light has a powerful effect on mood and reacts with biochemical agents and brain processes to regulate mood, with certain people being particularly sensitive to the relative darkness of autumn and winter. Fortunately for SAD sufferers the treatment of this condition is, compared with most other mental health problems, remarkably simple. Light boxes are available that can be placed on a desk and mimic the effect of daylight thus restoring biological balance and restoring the sufferer's mood, often without the need for anti-depressants. Unfortunately, other variants of depression are not explained so simply nor treated so effectively without the need for drugs or psychological therapy.

Infobox: Early warning signs

Episodes of depression or psychosis rarely happen 'out of the blue', and there are often subtle initial signs that a person is becoming psychotic. Sometimes the importance of such signs is only acknowledged by the sufferer and others who know them well. These are called 'early warning signs'. People usually have more than one early warning sign and they become increasingly evident as an individual becomes more unwell. The individual themselves may not be aware of these indicators and may deny them when discussed, but they should be reported to a GP or mental health professional when noticed. The person's care co-ordinator or a mental health professional should have a clear profile of early warning signs available, as should family, carers and the GP. There are a number of ways to identify early warning signs, but a profile can only be developed where there is a history of recurrent illness and the person concerned is reasonably well known to a health care professional. Some workers will utilise specific tools designed to identify early warning signs, although a simple list of relevant behaviours and/or feelings is normally sufficient, particularly for family and carers.

Common early warning signs include:

- sleep problems

- changes in appearance (e.g. wearing certain clothes, or becoming unusually smart or unkempt)

- fixation on subjects or objects (e.g. religion, politics, or a photograph)

- behaviour change (e.g. from sociable to quiet and withdrawn, or vice versa)

- feeling threatened without due cause

- irritability.

The individual profile of such signs will vary from person to person and may include any number of behaviours or feelings that history suggests are indicative of relapse.

Early warning signs are sometimes preceded by 'trigger factors', which might include insomnia (which may be either a trigger factor or an early warning sign), key dates or anniversaries, stress or non-compliance with medication. Awareness of trigger factors can prompt greater vigilance on the part of both the individual concerned and those around them.

CASENOTES: SEVERE MENTAL ILLNESS
Elizabeth

Elizabeth is 26 and has been living in a housing association flat for two years. She is from rural Yorkshire, but came to London after leaving home following many arguments about her odd behaviour. She has stayed with other family members for short periods of time, but either walked out or was asked to leave. She occasionally booked into night shelters or hostels, but her habits led to disputes with other residents and she would invariably move on elsewhere.

Elizabeth insists on washing her hands 24 times after using the toilet, or before eating. This is a carefully prepared ritual and can take up to an hour. She has always been very guarded about her reasons for doing this, but has disclosed to mental health professionals that if she does not do this she will catch Ebola and die. Elizabeth also insists on changing her shoes 24 times in any one 24-hour period (fortunately she has several pairs) and recites the Lord's Prayer 24 times at midnight every night.

One night while sleeping rough in London, Elizabeth was approached by police and asked to leave a public toilet in a train station following a complaint from a member of the public. She became aggressive and threatening, screaming at the police officers that if she could not wash herself 24 times she would die, and she would kill anyone who tried to prevent her. She was arrested and taken to a psychiatric unit, and subsequently detained under the Mental Health Act for further assessment when she refused to stay voluntarily. Elizabeth was dirty and dishevelled, carrying her belongings (including an assortment of shoes) in two carrier bags. She was isolated and withdrawn, refusing to talk to staff or other patients; it was noticed, however, that she appeared to be talking and laughing in her room although nobody was with her at the time.

Following a period of further assessment, and several altercations with other patients over her ritualistic behaviour, Elizabeth began to confide in one of the medical staff. The doctor found Elizabeth difficult to understand, but listened carefully to what she was saying and was able to reflect back to her one or two statements that were constantly repeated, mainly around the significance of the number '24' and her 'spiritual guides' who guided her actions and demanded complete obedience, which would be punished by infection with Ebola if she did not comply. Having spent several sessions with Elizabeth the doctor had learnt the names of the three spiritual guides and discovered that they sometimes spoke to her when she was alone, and although they were sometimes funny and made her laugh, they were usually rude and threatening.

The doctor empathised with Elizabeth, but suggested to her that her beliefs, and the voices of the spiritual guides, were probably the result of a severe mental illness that could be treated with medication. Elizabeth initially resisted this, and claimed that her voices had become even angrier with her for talking to a member of staff about them. However, she was eventually persuaded to try an anti-psychotic treatment, and was warned of possible side-effects and given a simple information sheet that explained how the drug worked.

Over the course of the next week, Elizabeth reported that the spiritual guides had become 'quieter' and she was not quite so afraid of them. She also became a little more communicative with others, although she still felt compelled to fulfil at least some of her rituals. She subsequently agreed to stay on the ward voluntarily and was taken off the section of the Mental Health Act. After several more weeks a Care Programme Approach (CPA) meeting was convened on the unit where she was introduced to staff from a local housing association. Elizabeth had agreed that they come to discuss accommodation at a mental health after-care hostel, and a plan of care was agreed for her discharge in a fortnight's time. A community psychiatric nurse was allocated to Elizabeth to act as her care co-ordinator after discharge.

In the meantime she visited the hostel and began to spend overnight stays there. After discharge from the psychiatric unit Elizabeth remained at the hostel for a further six months. During this time her hand-washing rituals and occasional truculence remained problematic for other residents and staff, and on several occasions she stopped taking medication and quickly became unwell again.

However, her care co-ordinator arranged for Elizabeth to attend a local support group for people suffering with psychotic illness, where Elizabeth learnt more about schizophrenia and the medication she was prescribed. Although she constantly complained that the medication 'drained her strength' and made her feel hungry all the time, she gradually learnt how the medication acted on her brain to correct some of the processes that could make her seriously ill. Elizabeth also enrolled at college to take the GCSEs she had failed while at school.

After the first six months at the hostel, Elizabeth was offered a flat managed by the housing association. This allowed her to carry out her rituals without bothering anyone else, and although her care co-ordinator suggested that she might be happier without the compulsion to wash her hands, Elizabeth flatly refused any further help, saying that her 'spiritual guides' had never really gone away, but were 'just lying low for the time being'.

Elizabeth: Points for reflection

1. What features can you identify that might suggest Elizabeth suffers from a psychotic illness?

2. What are her immediate needs prior to being admitted to hospital?

3. Why should Elizabeth require compulsory detention in hospital under the Mental Health Act?

4. Can you identify the most helpful aspects of Elizabeth's stay in hospital?

5. Can you identify the most helpful aspects of her aftercare and support following discharge from hospital?

Richard

Richard is usually a pleasant and gregarious character who keeps himself smart and tidy despite his unusual lifestyle. He can talk with some authority on literature and the arts, and is valued by other homeless people for his advice and help with completing forms and reading letters.

He was married for 13 years until the death of his wife from cancer. They had no children. Richard had run a successful printing business for many years prior to his wife's death, but found this increasingly difficult and sold it a year after his wife died. Within a very short period of time he had spent the proceeds of his business sale on a 'champagne' lifestyle of luxury cars, hotels and flights all over the world, and was eventually admitted to a psychiatric unit in France after running naked down the Champs-Élysées while singing 'Rule Britannia' through a megaphone.

He was transferred to a local unit, and settled quickly with medication, but attempted suicide shortly after being discharged and was readmitted. Richard left the hospital and disappeared. He sold his house and donated most of the money to various charities, placing a small amount in a trust fund from which he draws a weekly allowance. He has been living in various cities around the country, sleeping in his car and eating sandwiches and burgers.

Recently, Richard has become preoccupied with George Orwell's book *Down and Out in Paris and London* and is planning a return to Paris to live out his literary hero's life as a tramp. He has been discussing ways of drawing out all the remaining cash from his accounts and is hoping to hire a Santa Claus outfit and walk through the West End handing out 20-pound notes to anyone who appears to be in need.

Richard has not slept or eaten for several nights, and has been dressing in a variety of increasingly unusual outfits, which he changes several times a day. He has also been physically threatened by passers-by who have not appreciated his sudden and uninvited monologues on the works of obscure philosophers.

A homeless outreach team have managed to engage Richard and have tried, without success, to persuade him to come into hospital for a short time as they do not feel he is safe and believe that he is becoming increasingly overactive and bizarre. Richard is adamant that he will not come to hospital, and Approved Social Workers have failed to agree that his condition warrants detention under the Mental Health Act. However, Richard has said that he would agree to come to a staffed residential placement, and he has been referred to a hostel for a short while.

Richard: Points for reflection

1. Is Richard 'vulnerable', and if so, why?

2. Is Richard mentally ill, or just an eccentric and exceptionally generous man?

3. How might workers at the residential placement best offer support to Richard during his stay?

John

John is 72 years old and is a retired accountant. His wife Rose has asked their GP to visit at home as her husband has refused to get out of bed for several days and, according to Rose, has been 'peculiar' for the past three or four weeks.

When the GP arrives, John hides under the duvet and refuses to talk. The GP knows John well, and is puzzled by his behaviour as he is normally a sociable and humorous man in reasonably good health. When asked what she means by 'peculiar', Rose explains that her husband has become increasingly irritable and withdrawn, refusing to have anything to do with his children and grandchildren. Normally active and interested in sports and other hobbies, he had begun to watch television at all hours of the day and night, and seemed to have difficulty sleeping. His appetite had gradually disappeared and he had not eaten for several days.

When asked if she had ever noticed behaviour like this before, Rose explained that he used to become very stressed at work sometimes, but 'nothing a few pints and a round of golf with his mates wouldn't cure'. She had noticed that his alcohol consumption had increased gradually over the last few months, which he said was to help him sleep.

She also informed the doctor that John's mother had suffered from depression 'on and off' for many years, but this was something of a family secret and John did not like to discuss it. He was, she described, very much 'of the old school' and did not believe that personal problems should be discussed, even with family.

Rose appeared upset and angry toward her husband, and said that she had taken to sleeping in the spare room due to her husband's irritability and tendency to get up in the early hours of the morning for a glass of brandy.

The GP returned to her practice and made an urgent referral to the local Community Mental Health Team for assessment.

John: Points for reflection

1. Is John 'clinically' depressed, or he is just feeling miserable? What is the difference in this case?

2. John is a 72-year-old man. How might this affect his experience of depression, and others' ability to help him?

3. What are the potential risks involved should mental health professionals be unable to help John?

4. From the facts identified here, were there any early indications that John was becoming unwell?

References

Adams, B. (2002) *The Pits and the Pendulum: A Life with Bipolar Disorder*. London: Jessica Kingsley Publishers.

Ahmed, K. and Bhugra, D. (2007) 'Depression across ethnic minority cultures: Diagnostic issues.' *World Cultural Psychiatry Research Review 2*, 2/3, 47–56. Available at www.wcprr.org/pdf/02-23/2007.0203.4756.pdf.

Allen, P., Amaro, E., Fu, C.H., Williams, S.C., Brammer, M.J., Johns, L.C. and McGuire, P.K. (2007) 'Neural correlates of the misattribution of speech in schizophrenia.' *British Journal of Psychiatry 190*, 162–169.

American Psychiatric Association (2013) *Diagnostic and Statistical Manual of Mental Disorders* (5th Edition). Arlington, VA. American Psychiatric Publishing.

Anderson, I.M., Haddad, P.M. and Scott, J. (2012) 'Clinical review: Bipolar disorder.' *BMJ 345*, e8508.

Casadio, P., Fernandes, K., Murray, R.M. and Di Forti, M. (2011) 'Cannabis use in young people: The risk for schizophrenia.' *Neuroscience & Biobehavoral Reviews 35*, 8, 1779–1787. doi:10.1016/j.neubiorev.2011.04.007.

Craddock, N. and Owen, M. (2010) 'The Kraepelinian dichotomy – going, going… but still not gone.' *British Journal of Psychiatry 196*, 2, 92–95.

Crump, C., Sundquist, K., Winkleby, A.B. and Sundquist, J. (2010) 'Comorbidities and mortality in bipolar disorder: A Swedish national cohort study.' *JAMA Psychiatry 70*, 9, 931–939. doi:10.1001/jamapsychiatry.2013.1394.

Etain, B., Henry, C., Bellivier, F., Mathieu, F. and Leboyer, M. (2008) 'Beyond genetics: Childhood affective trauma in bipolar disorder.' *Bipolar Disorders 10*, 867–876.

Ferguson, D., Doucette, S., Glass, K.C., Shapiro, S. *et al.* (2005) 'Association between suicide attempts and selective serotonin reuptake inhibitors: Systematic review of randomised controlled trials.' *British Medical Journal 330*, 7488, 396.

Häfner, H. (2014) 'The concept of schizophrenia: From unity to diversity.' *Advances in Psychiatry*. doi:10.1155/2014/929434.

Haynes, J.C., Farrell, M., Singleton, N. *et al.* (2005) 'Alcohol consumption as a risk factor for anxiety and depression: Results from the longitudinal follow-up of the National Psychiatric Morbidity Survey.' *BJP 187*, 544–551.

Hor, K. and Taylor, M. (2010) 'Suicide and schizophrenia: A systematic review of rates and risk factors.' *Journal of Psychopharmacology 24*, 11, supplement 4, 81–90.

Kempton, M.J., Salvador, Z., Munafò, M.R. *et al.* (2011) 'Structural neuroimaging studies in major depressive disorder: Meta-analysis and comparison with bipolar disorder.' *Arch Gen Psychiatry 68,* 7, 675–690. doi:10.1001/archgenpsychiatry.2011.60.

Kinderman, P., Schwannauer, M., Pontin, E. and Tai, S. (2013) 'Psychological processes mediate the impact of familial risk, social circumstances and life events on mental health'. *PLoS One 8,* 10: e76564. doi:10.1371/journal/pone.0076564.

Laursen, T.M., Wahlbeck, K., Hällgren, J. *et al.* (2013) 'Life expectancy and death by diseases of the circulatory system in patients with bipolar disorder or schizophrenia in the Nordic countries.' *PLoS One 8,* 6: e67133. doi:10.1371/journal.pone.0067133.

Marazziti, D., Akiskal, H., Rossi, A. and Cassano, G. (1999) 'Alteration of the platelet serotonin transporter in romantic love.' *Psychological Medicine 29,* 3, 741–745.

McGrath, J., Saha, S., Chant, D. and Welham, J. (2008) 'Schizophrenia: A concise overview of incidence, prevalence, and mortality.' *Epidemiologic Reviews 30,* 67–76. doi:10.1093/epirev/mxn001.

McManus, S., Meltzer, H., Brugha, T., Bebbington, P. and Jenkins, R. (2009) *Adult Psychiatric Morbidity in England, 2007: Results of a Household Survey.* London: National Centre for Social Research. Available at www.hscic.gov.uk/catalogue/PUB02931/adul-psyc-morb-res-hou-sur-eng-2007-rep.pdf.

Menezes, N.M., Arenovich, T. and Zipursky, R.B. (2006) 'A systematic review of longitudinal outcome studies of first-episode psychosis.' *Psychological Medicine 36,* 10, 1349–1362.

Moghaddam, B. and Javitt, D. (2012) 'From revolution to evolution: The glutamate hypothesis of schizophrenia and its implication for treatment.' *Neuropsychopharmacology Reviews 37,* 1, 4–15. doi:10.1038/npp.2011.181.

NHS (2014) *Five steps to mental wellbeing.* Available at www.nhs.uk/Conditions/stress-anxiety-depression/Pages/improve-mental-wellbeing.aspx.

NICE (2003) *Guidance on the Use of Electroconvulsive Therapy.* Technology Appraisal No. 59. London: National Institute for Clinical Excellence.

NICE (2014) *Bipolar Disorder: The Assessment and Management of Bipolar Disorder in Adults, Children and Young People in Primary and Secondary Care.* NICE Clinical Guideline 185. London: National Institute for Health and Care Excellence. Available at www.nice.org.uk/guidance/cg185.

Nordentoft, M., Mortensen, P.B. and Pedersen, C.B. (2011) 'Absolute risk of suicide after first hospital contact in mental disorder.' *Archives of General Psychiatry 68,* 1058–1064.

Odegaard, O. (1932) 'Emigration and insanity: A study of mental disease among the Norwegian born population of Minnesota.' *Acta Psychiatrica et Neurologica Scandinavica 7*, Supplement 4, 1–206.

Owen, M., O'Donovan, M. and Harrison, P. (2005) 'Schizophrenia: A genetic disorder of the synapse?' *British Medical Journal 330*, 158–159.

Patel, V. (2001) 'Cultural factors and international epidemiology.' *Br Med Bull 57*, 33–45.

Power, R.A., Verweij, J.H., Zuhair, M., Montgomery, G.W. *et al.* (2014) 'Genetic predisposition to schizophrenia associated with increased use of cannabis.' *Molecular Psychiatry 19*, 1201–1204.

Reid, S. and Barbui, C. (2010) 'Long term treatment of depression with selective serotonin reuptake inhibitors and newer antidepressants.' *BMJ 340*, c1468.

Shiers, D. and Curtis, J. (2014) 'Cardiometabolic health in young people with psychosis.' *Lancet Psychiatry.* doi:10.1016/S2215-0366(14)00072-8.

Smoller, J.W., Craddock, N., Kendler, K., Lee, P.H. *et al.* (2013) 'Identification of risk loci with shared effects on five major psychiatric disorders: A genome-wide analysis.' *Lancet 381*, 9875, 1371–1379.

Time to Change (2014) *Attitudes to Mental Illness 2013: Research Report.* London: TNS BMRB. Available at www.time-to-change.org.uk/sites/default/files/121168_Attitudes_to_mental_illness_2013_report.pdf.

Van Os, J. and Kapur, S. (2009) 'Schizophrenia.' *Lancet 374*, 9690, 635–645. doi: 10.1016/S0140-6736(09)60995-8.

World Health Organization (1992) *ICD-10: Classification of Mental and Behavioural Disorders.* Geneva: WHO.

World Health Organization (2009) *Global Health Risks: Mortality and Burden of Disease Attributable to Selected Major Risks.* Geneva: WHO.

Chapter 2

TREATMENT AND SUPPORT

At 10am on Saturday 19 January 1952 a distressed and highly agitated young Parisian was administered a 50 mg dose of a new compound called chlorpromazine. Within 20 days 'Jacques Lh' was reported by his doctors to be ready for 'normal life' (Ban 2007).

This proved to be the genesis of a new era of psychiatric treatment. At roughly the same time in the United States, doctors experimenting with new anti-tubercolosis drugs noticed an interesting side-effect. Patients presented with pronounced (and at times 'inappropriate') mood elevation after taking isoniazid and iproniazid. Within a few years anti-depressants were in common use alongside the new anti-psychotic medications. The use (and abuse) of medication in mental health care remains a contested issue, but few would argue that the advent of this new and relatively scientific approach to treating mental illness represented an enormous leap in the humane treatment of conditions such as schizophrenia and depression.

For hundreds of years, the mentally ill were categorised as 'lunatic' or 'melancholic' and locked away, often in chains and with no means of treating their distress. Eventually the growing science of psychiatry began experimenting with new 'treatments', which were at best non-effective, and at worst horrific. Ice baths, induced comas, ECT (without anaesthetic or muscle relaxants), insulin shock and brain surgery were commonplace attempts by medical psychiatry to introduce the notion of 'treatment' into the care of the mentally ill; but death, illness and severe personality change were more likely effects of these dubious practices than any improvement in mental health.

Nowadays the true efficacy of most of the drugs used in psychiatry is often questioned. Vast amounts of anti-depressants are prescribed throughout the developed world, often inappropriately and for conditions known not to respond well to drugs such as fluoxetine. Anti-psychotics receive their share of criticism, mainly as we still know relatively little about how they actually work, and also because their effect is limited to controlling certain features of psychotic illness without actually 'curing' the illness. Nonetheless, the treatment of severe depression and conditions such as bipolar disorder or schizophrenia has been revolutionised by these developments, and much of the current work on the causes and nature of severe mental illness will inevitably lead to drug treatments that are much more tightly focused on the individual symptoms and problems than the current group of medications.

Medication

Psychiatric drugs have attracted few plaudits in recent years. As we have seen in the previous chapter, the cause and effect of mental disorder is only now beginning to be understood with any degree of precision. Patients are often reluctant to take medication (Morrison *et al.* 2014), and drugs such as anti-psychotics and anti-depressants have only a limited effect for a significant proportion of those who take them. Nonetheless, with careful prescribing and administration, anti-psychotics, tranquillisers, anti-depressants and others do have a valuable role to play in mental health care alongside the support of family, friends and professionals, and some of the 'talking treatments' we shall be looking at later in this chapter.

Most of the drugs used specifically in mental health care can be classified on belonging to one of several main groups. As if the huge variety of drugs, dosages and preparations were not confusing enough, medicines are usually known by (a) 'brand' names or proprietary names and (b) generic names. For example, Prozac is now one of the best-known drugs in the world, but very few people would recognise the same preparation by its generic title 'fluoxetine'.

Pharmacists, prescribers and mental health professionals are generally encouraged to use the generic names of drugs as one preparation may have more than one brand name, particularly if it has been on the market for more than a few years. We shall use this section of the chapter to outline some of the main types of medication used in mental health care to treat severe mental illness.

Anti-psychotic medication
TYPICAL ANTI-PSYCHOTICS

Rather misleadingly, the 'typical' anti-psychotics are often referred to as 'major tranquillisers'. This group of drugs is designed to target the areas of the brain responsible for psychotic phenomena such as thought disorder, hallucinations, and so on. Chlorpromazine, the first anti-psychotic drug, was first used in the 1950s and preceded a number of other anti-psychotic drugs that worked by blocking some of the brain's dopamine receptors, reducing the concentration of this chemical and reducing some of the more distressing symptoms of psychotic illness. The so-called 'typical' anti-psychotics first discovered in the 1950s were used for several decades with good enough effects to allow the closure of the old asylums and the advent of community care. But one serious drawback of the typical anti-psychotics is their tendency to cause serious side-effects, such as sedation and problems with mobility. Typical anti-psychotics are effective at blocking some of the mechanisms of distressing symptoms, including thought disorder and hallucinations, but the relief of psychosis can come at a high price.

Typical anti-psychotics also have quite powerful sedative effects, and are sometimes used for this purpose for people whose symptoms lead to restlessness, agitation or aggression, hence the term 'major tranquillisers'. In less acute circumstances however, the sedation caused by chlorpromazine or haloperidol combined with the low mood, apathy and social withdrawal often associated with mental illness is obviously less than desirable, and is a major cause of non-compliance with drug treatment. Chlorpromazine, sulpiride and haloperidol are all examples of tablet form anti-psychotics, but several of these drugs are given as depot injections and release their effects very gradually. This is a type of medication often given to patients who have difficulties taking tablets, or who are non-adherent and may need some form of legal or coercive procedure to be given regular depot injections.

ATYPICAL ANTI-PSYCHOTICS

These drugs operate in much the same way as the 'typical' anti-psychotics, but are more precise in the way they reduce excess dopamine and other neurotransmitters, such as serotonin. They are on the whole less sedating than their typical predecessors, and are effective for most people in lessening or removing altogether the effect of troubling psychotic phenomena such as voices or paranoia. Some of the atypical anti-psychotic drugs also help counter the 'negative' symptoms of schizophrenia, including social withdrawal and apathy.

Drugs such as risperidone, olanzapine and the injectable aripiprazole have become the drugs of choice for the short- and long-term treatment of psychotic illness, and have contributed to a lower incidence of the side-effects that became synonymous with the shuffling, unsteady gait of many patients from the old asylums. Weight gain remains a particular problem with many of the atypical drugs, as well as an increased risk of diabetes and heart irregularities.

Clozapine is an atypical anti-psychotic that was first used to treat schizophrenia only several years after the discovery of chlorpromazine. However, while it is highly effective in treating severe mental illness it can cause side-effects such as weight gain, seizures or a blood disorder called neutropenia, which reduces a person's ability to fight infection. For this reason its use is reserved for people who have not responded to, or are intolerant of, other treatments and requires regular blood testing and very careful management by doctors and mental health professionals.

Anxiolytics

The term 'anxiolytic' is usually used to refer to any drug treatment aimed at reducing anxiety. Of course, as anyone who has tried public speaking will testify, anxiety is a very normal and usually short-lived reaction to stressful events. But for some people, anxiety is a chronic, debilitating problem that prevents the sufferer from performing even everyday tasks. Anxiolytics are often confused with 'tranquillisers', although some of the drugs listed here could not be described as tranquillisers in the normal sense.

BENZODIAZEPINES

Drugs such as diazepam or lorazepam are among the best-known anxiolytics and belong to a class of drugs known as benzodiazepines. Often referred to as 'benzos' by drug addicts, and 'minor tranquillisers' by mental health professionals, drugs such as diazepam are quite sought after as drugs of abuse, and their rapid effect and potential for creating dependence make the benzodiazepines anything but 'minor'.

Patients develop 'tolerance' to benzodiazepines quite quickly, requiring larger doses over time in order to gain the same calming effect. Nonetheless, prescribed responsibly and over a short period of time the benzodiazepines offer useful quick-acting sedation for people in severe distress and anxiety, allowing the potential for the person to discuss their feelings and talk through the problems that have caused the distress before their situation becomes uncontrollable. Drugs such as chlordiazepoxide have long provided a mainstay of treatment for those undergoing detoxification from alcohol.

OTHER ANXIOLYTICS

Beta-blockers such as propanolol and oxprenolol are better known as 'blood pressure tablets' than anxiolytics, and are usually prescribed to people with hypertension or cardiac problems. However, they are sometimes useful in the treatment of anxiety, particularly as they are in many ways less harmful than the benzodiazepines. They work by 'damping down' the physical effects of adrenaline and noradrenaline (the 'fight, flight and fright' hormones) and therefore reducing the psychological effects of anxiety.

We should also mention another anxiolytic called buspirone, which belongs to a class of drug known as the 'azaspirodecanediones'. We needn't worry to much about the latter or try to pronounce it, suffice to say that buspirone depresses anxiety on a long-term basis in a way not dissimilar to the SSRI anti-depressants (see below) and is not normally dependence-inducing like the benzodiazepines.

Anti-depressants

As the name suggests, an anti-depressant is a drug used in combating the most debilitating effects of clinical depression. Contrary to some beliefs, anti-depressants are not 'happy pills' and have no 'street' or recreational value. They have been shown to have little effect for treating milder forms of depression, but are generally successful at reducing the symptoms of more severe depressive illness (NICE 2009). They are of little use in cases of short-term grief or as 'pick-me-ups' for adverse events as they take several weeks to have any demonstrable effect, but can be invaluable in situations where the symptoms of depression have prevented an individual from leading a normal life.

There are, broadly speaking, two main classes of anti-depressant commonly prescribed by GPs and psychiatrists: tricyclic anti-depressants and SSRIs (selective serotonin reuptake inhibitors).

TRICYCLIC ANTI-DEPRESSANTS

Tricyclic anti-depressants have been available for many years, and work on making more of the neurotransmitters serotonin and noradrenaline available, both of which are important in regulating mood. However, tricyclics take a rather indiscriminate approach to chemical regulation and can cause quite pronounced drowsiness and symptoms of dehydration (e.g. blurred vision and dry mouth). Some tricyclics, such as amitriptyline or imipramine are also known to be dangerous in overdose, and many prescribers now prefer to use the SSRI-type drugs (see below) to treat depression.

SELECTIVE SEROTONIN REUPTAKE INHIBITORS (SSRIS)

While working in much the same way as the tricyclics, the SSRIs are more (as the name suggests) selective in the way they work and some SSRIs also affect neurotransmitters such as noradrenaline and other brain pathways. These drugs are generally less toxic in overdose, and patients report fewer and less severe side-effects. Like the tricyclics, benefits depend on a certain therapeutic level of the drug building up in the patient's bloodstream, and positive effects will not usually be seen for several weeks following the first dose. The widespread and sometimes inappropriate prescribing of some SSRIs has attracted criticism in the UK, particularly with regard to the number of children and adolescents now prescribed SSRI drugs, a practice that is now tightly regulated (MHPRA 2004).

Paroxetine has gained a certain notoriety for allegedly causing dependence and behaviour change in patients. It is sometimes difficult to distinguish the perceived negative effects of a psychoactive drug from the symptoms of mental disorder itself, a fact that has complicated the research into the potentially harmful effects of drugs such as paroxetine and fluoxetine. While prescribing safeguards are now beginning to appear in legislation, it should also be remembered that SSRIs are taken effectively and without problem by many thousands of people throughout the world (National Collaborating Centre for Mental Health 2004).

Mood stabilisers

People with bipolar disorder are usually treated with drugs to help stabilise the extremes of mood (mania and depression) that characterise this illness. They are not a 'cure' for bipolar disorder but are helpful in maintaining stability, or what mental health professionals call a 'baseline mental state'. Studies have shown that extremes of mood and relapse are much more common when sufferers remain untreated; although, as we have already seen, diagnosis is often difficult and compliance with medication is sometimes compromised by the symptoms of the illness itself and the unsurprising reluctance of many bipolar sufferers to submit themselves to lifelong medication (Sajatovic *et al.* 2007).

Mood stabilisers do not belong to any particular chemical type. Two of the most commonly used treatments are better known as anti-epileptic drugs, and perhaps the best known, lithium, is actually a metal. The atypical anti-psychotic olanzapine has recently been licensed in the UK as a mood stabiliser. The dissimilarity of the drugs used to treat bipolar disorder reflect the vagaries of the illness itself, and prescribers need to carefully control or 'titrate' doses and medications in accordance with the nature of the patient's illness. Furthermore, combinations of different mood stabilisers may sometimes need to be prescribed where one medication, or 'monotherapy' is not maintaining stability alone.

Lithium in particular needs careful monitoring. In high concentrations it can be toxic and its levels are measured by regular blood tests. Patients are advised not to become dehydrated (a particular risk for heavy drinkers) and to take medical advice before taking other prescribed or 'over-the-counter' medicines. Any signs of physical ill-health in patients taking lithium should be reported to health professionals immediately.

Talking treatments

Where mental health services are either rapidly diminishing (in the UK) or were never available in the first place (the developing world), medication provides a relatively cheap and simple solution to complex problems that are otherwise resource-hungry and time-consuming. Nonetheless, there are now a number of well-evidenced, effective therapies and supports for people with mental illness. Some of the more ubiquitous examples are outlined here.

Cognitive behaviour therapy (CBT)

The basis of CBT is that an individual's thoughts, feelings and behaviour are closely linked, and that if we can change the way a person thinks then we can also alter and improve the way they feel and what they do. CBT has been found to be as effective a treatment for mild to moderate depression as anti-depressant drugs. But CBT has in recent years extended its range to the successful treatment of people with psychotic illnesses and positive symptoms such as auditory hallucinations (Kuipers 2006).

CBT challenges a person's negative core beliefs. Depressed patients may believe that every ill that befalls their family is their fault. People with schizophrenia may believe their thoughts are being broadcast on Facebook.

These core beliefs dramatically affect an individual's day-to-day life, but a cognitive therapist makes detailed records of a person's thoughts, beliefs and actions and helps the patient challenge these, with the ultimate aim of dispelling and replacing negative thoughts, feelings and behaviours with more positive versions of the same.

Cognitive behaviour therapy is quite different from many other types of therapy in that it is short term, highly focused and deals more with the 'here and now' rather than concentrating on links with the past or attempting to explain 'why' the patient feels a certain way. CBT has also shown encouraging results through the development of increasingly sophisticated online versions, which will of course make therapy widely and very cheaply available for people not requiring more intensive 1:1 support.

Counselling/psychotherapy

There are dozens of different forms and theories of counselling and psychotherapy. The easiest description of counselling is that it is a process of spending time with another person and perhaps helping them find their own solutions to one or more difficult issues. Therefore most people probably engage in some form of counselling on an informal, day-to-day basis, whether with clients, friends or members of the family.

Most carers and mental health professionals use basic counselling skills in their work with clients, although very few have a specific qualification. Professional counsellors and psychotherapists have studied for several years, and have often undergone therapy themselves as part of their training. In practice, there is a great deal of overlap between professional counselling and psychotherapy, although most practitioners would suggest that counselling focuses on specific issues (such as bereavement or addiction) whilst psychotherapy is a more 'in-depth' process of self-discovery.

People in distress can often get significant benefit from talking to a trusted individual who has the ability to 'actively listen' to what they have to say. This is, in effect, counselling. It doesn't necessarily require 'knowing what to say' or making insightful interpretations of a person's behaviour, as it is the counsellor's role to help the person find their own solutions, not give advice.

Early intervention for psychosis

It has been well known for a number of years that a positive prognosis of psychotic illness, and schizophrenia in particular, depends to a large extent on promptness of intervention as soon as possible after symptoms emerge (Marshall *et al.* 2005).

Early intervention services are now widespread throughout the UK. Teams may operate independently or form part of a multi-disciplinary team, and focus on the identification of very early signs of impending psychotic illness in (mainly young) people.

Early intervention teams work holistically with 'first episode' patients in terms of social and family support, low-dose medication, and the increasingly important monitoring of physical health, which is now known to be severely compromised by psychotic illness, particularly at an early stage of the illness (Shiers and Curtis 2014).

──────── *Infobox: Electro-convulsive therapy* ────────

Prior to the advent of the major tranquillisers, and more sophisticated talking treatments such as cognitive behaviour therapy (CBT), the 'treatment' of mental health problems ranged from the bizarre to the positively dangerous. Most 'treatment' was of a physical nature and included cold baths, insulin-induced comas or padded cells and strait-jackets. Electro-convulsive therapy (ECT) has its origins in that era although it is used on a strictly 'last resort' basis and is today a carefully monitored medical treatment rather than the unsophisticated and painful procedure of several decades ago.

ECT involves the passing of a small electric current through the brain to relieve symptoms of depression and, occasionally, psychotic illness. The process is strictly controlled and administered under general anaesthetic and muscle-relaxant drugs.

The anaesthetised patient experiences brief seizures before being brought back to consciousness under close medical supervision. ECT is usually prescribed only when the patient's symptoms have not responded to more conventional treatments such as anti-depressant medication.

Despite the closely supervised nature and safeguards (National Institute for Clinical Excellence 2003), not to mention its reputation for bringing about rapid improvement in severely depressed people, ECT remains controversial and is still regarded by some as an instrument of torture rather than a bona fide medical treatment befitting the 21st century. The arguments surrounding the use of ECT are also fuelled by the fact that little information exists as to how it works, and side-effects of the treatment often include loss of memory (which is not normally permanent) and short-term disorientation. Most (but not all) mental health professionals regard ECT as an

> effective treatment where the patient is dangerously unwell or where he or she has failed to respond to more conventional treatments such as anti-depressant medication.

The Professionals: Health, social and the non-statutory services

Mental health care in the UK is carried out by a wide variety of organisations, some of whom are 'statutory' (i.e. provided and managed by the National Health Service or local authority) and some of whom are 'non-statutory' or 'voluntary'. Examples of the latter group might be charities or housing associations who provide services for mentally ill people independently of 'the state', although they will usually complement and work closely with the statutory services and will have to work within a legal framework such as the Registered Care Homes Act.

The Community Mental Health Team (CMHT)

In this section we are going to focus on those statutory services that are responsible for most 'front-line' mental health care in the community: the Community Mental Health Team or CMHT. All the professions outlined here will also feature in hospital-based mental health care although most individual practitioners tend to be based in either in-patient or community settings, and form part of what is known as a 'secondary care' service (see Infobox on the following page).

Infobox: The NHS and mental health
– primary, secondary or tertiary?

The NHS can be seen as a three-tier process comprising three distinct layers: primary, secondary and tertiary care.

Primary health care

The primary health care system is the network of general practice surgeries serving local communities. A practice usually includes at least one GP together with a variety of other health care professionals (such as practice nurses, physiotherapists, chiropodists, etc.) providing treatments and other medical services. Some (but by no means all) practices employ community psychiatric nurses (CPNs) and qualified counsellors.

Primary health currently provides a substantial proportion of mental health care for those with less severe disorders. Counsellors and CPNs may see patients referred by their GPs suffering anxiety or depression of a type that does not necessarily warrant intervention from a Community Mental Health Team (CMHT). The Improving Access to Psychological Therapies service now see (despite reportedly long waiting lists) the majority of people referred with these issues, using very structured and time-limited applications of cognitive behaviour therapy to help people with troublesome but less severe mental health issues. Some patients prefer to be treated purely by their own GPs, who often prescribe anxiolytics or anti-depressants while monitoring a patient's symptoms over a period of time, only referring to more specialist assessment in cases where the situation worsens or problems remain intractable for substantial periods of time.

Secondary health care

Secondary health care is the terminology applied to specialist treatments usually provided by a hospital or clinic. A GP refers to a specialist in secondary health care for more detailed assessment or specialist treatment such as surgery. CMHTs form part of the secondary health care system, as do in-patient psychiatric units and hospitals.

Tertiary health care

'Tertiary' refers to the most specialised level of care, examples of which include services such as eating disorder teams, or forensic psychiatric services, which work with mentally disordered offenders.

The CMHT is a multi-disciplinary team usually comprising a core group of professionals such as psychiatrists, nurses, social workers, clinical psychologists and occupational therapists. Not all teams work in the same way, and other workers often form part of the team to provide practical support and assistance to both patients and qualified staff, or may lead specific projects such as job clubs, cafés, horticultural nurseries or painting and decorating groups.

Each CMHT will cover a locality designated as a defined area on a map, or as a collection of GP surgeries. The way in which local CMHTs work will vary widely from team to team and area to area depending on the nature of the catchment area. For example, a rural CMHT will usually cover a wide geographical area and may work in a very different way to a team based in a densely populated urban area. Local demographic factors such as affluence, age and ethnicity will also influence working practices, so it is very difficult to describe the 'typical' CMHT as they are far from homogeneous! One feature virtually all team members share is their responsibility to act as 'care co-ordinator' under the auspices of the Care Programme Approach (see Infobox below). While CMHT patients may be involved with several different professions at any one time, their keyworker acts as the main point of contact for that person and will be responsible for preparing and facilitating a plan of care for each patient on their caseload.

There are many myths and misunderstandings surrounding the roles of the various mental health professionals, and this section outlines the roles and responsibilities of the various disciplines. It should be point out that some teams work with professionals whose boundaries are very clear, while others take a more 'generic' approach where all team members undertake a variety of tasks within the team more or less irrespective of their professional background.

─────*Infobox: The Care Programme Approach*─────

The Care Programme Approach (CPA) was introduced in 1991 by an Act of Parliament the previous year (Community Care Act 1990) and is intended to be the basis for the care of people with mental health needs outside hospital. It applies to all people with mental health problems who are accepted as clients of specialist mental health services.

In many cases, the CPA comes into play while someone is a psychiatric hospital in-patient (not necessarily detained under the Mental Health Act), and creates the framework for discharge planning and aftercare. The CPA also links in with care management practised by local authority social services departments, where social services departments are undertaking their duties of assessing needs and purchasing appropriate services, under the NHS and Community Care Act. CPA, care management and (where applicable) section 117 duties (see Chapter 7) can be integrated into a single process.

The CPA process has four stages:

- a systematic assessment of the person's health care and social care needs

- the development of a care plan agreed by all involved, including the person her/himself and any informal carers, as far as this is possible, and addressing the assessed needs

- identifying a keyworker to be the main point of contact with the person concerned and to monitor the delivery of the care plan

- regular review of the person's progress and the care plan, with agreed changes to the plan as required.

THE PSYCHIATRIST

A psychiatrist is a medically qualified doctor who has undertaken several years further training in psychiatry. To specialise in this field a psychiatrist will have qualified for membership of the Royal College of Psychiatrists. Most (but not all) CMHTs are led by a consultant psychiatrist and will have responsibility for diagnosis, pharmacological treatment and overall management of patient care. Like other mental health professionals, a psychiatrist might practise as a general clinician while others may undertake further specialist training in areas such as eating disorders, forensic psychiatry (the assessment and treatment of mentally disordered offenders) or child and adolescent mental health.

Unlike other members of the team, psychiatrists will usually work in both in-patient and community settings, and may often have an allocated number of beds at a psychiatric unit to which they can admit patients.

Most of the powers to detain individuals under the Mental Health Act require a doctor's assessment, although those parts of the Act which determine compulsory treatment must be sanctioned by a psychiatrist specially approved under section 12 of the Mental Health Act (see Chapter 7). If the patient is subject to the Mental Health Act, the 'Responsible Medical Officer' has a legal as well as clinical responsibility, including decisions around the detention, discharge and leave accorded to the patient.

Psychiatrists are often portrayed in the media as 'talking therapists' who see their patients on couches and make interpretations of their behaviour based on childhood events. In reality, while some psychiatrists are trained in various 'talking treatments', most perform much the same role as doctors in other medical specialisms in that they diagnose mental health problems and prescribe an appropriate course of treatment if necessary.

THE CLINICAL PSYCHOLOGIST

Trained psychologists exist in many guises. Some remain within the academic world after graduating and conduct research studies on how the human mind thinks, feels, reacts and makes decisions, or how individuals perform within groups or how groups interact with other groups. Much of our current understanding of mental disorder comes from the field of neuro-psychology, where responses and actions are compared with detailed 'real-time' brain scanning. Psychologists also work in business, industry, advertising and sport, but a 'clinical' psychologist treats patients and works directly with mental health problems using a variety of specialised techniques. They are skilled in the use of a range of diagnostic tests and tools, and may carry out a wide range of treatments, particularly the 'talking treatments' we have looked at earlier. Clinical psychologists also provide training and supervision in this kind of work to other professionals.

Clinical psychologists are often confused with psychiatrists, especially by the media. Sometimes a clinical psychologist will have a post-graduate research degree such as a PhD and will therefore have the prefix 'Dr', but is not qualified in medicine. Clinical psychologists must have a degree in psychology plus a further qualification in clinical work.

THE COMMUNITY PSYCHIATRIC NURSE (CPN)

Community psychiatric nurses (CPNs) are qualified mental health nurses, some of whom have completed specialist training for community work. Most CMHTs include several CPNs, which form the most numerous workforce of all the disciplines. They work in an increasingly wide range of situations with a diverse patient group. Some work with patients referred by a local GP, others work within substance dependence clinics, with the street homeless, or in prisons. They are responsible for helping patients with practical problems, and are often qualified in delivering different types of therapy such as behaviour therapy or counselling.

They are sometimes responsible for both the administration and management of medicines (particularly the depot anti-psychotics outlined earlier) and helping patients understand both their diagnosis and the treatment they are receiving.

THE MENTAL HEALTH SOCIAL WORKER

Social workers are another professional group whose role is often misunderstood. The mental health social worker (MHSW) is a key member of the CMHT although, unlike many of their colleagues, he or she is usually employed by the local authority rather then the local NHS Trust.

MHSWs have a general qualification in social work and have specialised later in mental health. They co-ordinate and monitor care plans, and are often responsible for managing and budgeting for a complete package of care, including services such as housing, work retraining and benefits advice. Their training and work experience often leads to work with families, where one family member's mental health problems may be leading to problems within the family as a whole, or where the family are acting as 'carers' and require support to carry out this role.

THE OCCUPATIONAL THERAPIST

Occupational therapists undergo three years' training prior to qualification and work in a range of settings beyond mental health. Their role within the multi-disciplinary team is to assess a patient's skills and functioning using specific tools, and based on that assessment develop occupational treatment programmes. The programmes are regularly reviewed to measure changes in the patient's functioning and are adapted accordingly.

For some people with an enduring mental illness such as depression or schizophrenia, isolation and loss of motivation are key issues along with impaired ability to carry out everyday tasks such as cooking, shopping, going to work or looking after a house.

Occupational therapy helps clients to improve skills they may have lost due to illness, and to develop coping strategies for returning to a more normal way of life.

Non-statutory services

Large psychiatric hospitals (or 'asylums') have been in the process of closing down since the early 1960s, with the 1990 Community Care Act accelerating the process to the point that today's mental health care is largely delivered in the patient's own locality.

Many of the services once provided solely by health and social services professionals are now delivered by a wide variety of organisations. In particular, a number of charities and special needs housing associations offer support, advice and practical help in addition to meeting basic needs such as housing. These agencies are now working closely with the statutory sector (health and social services) and in many cases receive the bulk of their funding from government and local authorities. Examples of services provided by non-statutory agencies include housing, day care, employment schemes, advice centres and telephone helplines.

References

Ban, T.A. (2007) 'Fifty years chlorpromazine: A historical perspective.' *Neuropsychiatric Disease and Treatment 3*, 4, 495–500.

Kuipers, E., Garety, P., Fowler, D., Freeman, D., Dunn, G. and Bebbington, P. (2006) 'Cognitive, emotional, and social processes in psychosis: Refining cognitive behavioral therapy for persistent positive symptoms.' *Schizophrenia Bulletin 32*, S1, S24–S31.

Marshall, M., Lewis, S., Lockwood, A., Drake, R., Jones, P. and Croudace, T. (2005) 'Association between duration of untreated psychosis and outcome in cohorts of first-episode patients: A systematic review.' *Archives of General Psychiatry 62*, 9, 975–983.

Medicines and Healthcare Products Regulatory Agency (2004) *Report of the CSM Expert Working Group on the Safety of Selective Serotonin Reuptake Inhibitor Antidepressants.* Available at www.mhra.gov.uk/home/groups/pl-p/documents/drugsafetymessage/con019472.pdf.

Morrison, A.P., Turkington, D., Pyle, M., Spencer, H. *et al.* (2014) 'Cognitive therapy for people with schizophrenia spectrum disorders not taking antipsychotic drugs: A single blind randomised controlled trial.' *Lancet 383*, 9926, 1395–1403.

National Collaborating Centre for Mental Health (2004) *Depression: Management of Depression in Primary and Secondary Care.* Clinical Guideline 23. London: National Institute for Clinical Excellence.

NICE (2009) *Depression in Adults: The Treatment and Management of Depression in Adults.* NICE Clinical Guideline 90. London: National Institute for Health and Clinical Excellence. Available at www.nice.org.uk/guidance/cg90.

Sajatovic, M., Valenstein, M., Blow, F., Ganoczy, D. and Ignacio. R. (2007) 'Treatment adherence with lithium and anticonvulsant medications among patients with bipolar disorder.' *Psychiatric Services 58*, 855–863.

Shiers, D. and Curtis, J. (2014) 'Cardiometabolic health in young people with psychosis.' *Lancet Psychiatry.* doi:10.1016/S2215-0366(14)00072-8.

Sørensen, R., Høifødta, C., Strømb, N., Kolstrupb, M., Eisemanna, M. and Waterlooa, K. (2011) 'Effectiveness of cognitive behavioural therapy in primary health care: A review.' *Family Practice 28*, 5, 489–504.

Chapter 3

RISK ASSESSMENT AND MANAGEMENT

In its broadest sense, the term 'risk' represents the delicate balance between the potential benefit of a proposed action and the potential harm that action may cause. In mental health terms, this means providing service users with as much choice, freedom and opportunity as possible while being aware that people with mental health problems do sometimes harm themselves or other people. Mental health carers are daily charged with the responsibility of using the evidence available to us to balance opportunities against threat, and to work with service users on a plan of care that reflects this.

Most mentally ill people will not cause serious harm to themselves or others. They are in fact more likely to be the victims of violence than the general population (Hughes *et al.* 2012). Campaigns such as Time to Think have worked hard to dispel the 'danger myth' that surrounds the mentally ill. Charities, user groups and mental health professionals are also forced to remind a disbelieving public that violent crime is overwhelmingly committed by people with no history of mental health problems beyond a predilection for super strength lager.

Nonetheless, suicide, self-injury, self-neglect and violence to others are events common enough to concern most social care and mental health services.

For those of us who wish to learn from the past to inform current and future practice, there now exists a vast library of inquiries and reports into tragedies that have occurred (to at least some degree) as a result of mental ill health. Independent inquiries into the circumstances of 'patient' homicides (i.e. where the perpetrator has had some contact with psychiatric services prior to the offence) have now been mandatory for many years. In December 1992, a musician called Jonathan Zito was fatally stabbed on the platform of a London tube station by one Christopher Clunis. The subsequent independent inquiry into the events that led up to the killing (Ritchie, Dick and Lingham 1994) was the first of what has become a mandatory requirement for such homicides. The Ritchie Report, as it became known, identified a catalogue of poor judgement, poor communication and what can only be described as 'buck passing' by a spread of agencies all having some contact with Christopher Clunis prior to the tragedy. The inquiry revealed a man who was himself tormented by psychosis but whose very obvious need for support was overlooked, missed or passed on by community services and mental health professionals.

Unfortunately, the findings of this and many, many reports that have followed appear not to have informed a practice of risk assessment and management that should be, when practised by well-trained practitioners with clear procedures and aims, a process of achieving balance between safety on the one hand and quality of life on the other. With the application of some basic skills in the assessment and management of risk, workers can at least make an informed decision as to the likelihood and severity of untoward events, and care plans can be developed that allow events such as these to happen as seldom as possible within the resources available.

Many individuals will present no form of risk at all, and the thorough processes described here may appear superfluous. But for people who are known to have been aggressive, suicidal or to have put themselves at risk through a worsening of their mental state or erratic lifestyle, risk assessment and management is an undoubtedly essential aspect of our overall care.

This part of the book is an attempt to outline some of the most important principles in risk assessment and management. It is by necessity generic, as every organisation will have developed their own policies and procedures in assessing and managing risk. The guidance offered here is broad-ranging but based on good practice and sound evidence, intended to suggest good practice rather than propose any specific framework.

What is risk assessment?

The assessment of risk involves the identification of factors and circumstances that may contribute to an untoward incident or situation. The aim is to avoid harm to both the service user or other persons, which may come in the form of self-harm, suicide, violence toward others, self-neglect or exploitation.

A car driver's insurance premiums may be calculated on the basis of precise mathematical formulae, but mental health risk assessment is not a statistical process. It is impossible to predict with accuracy the probability that Client A will perform Action X within a given period of time. But through a process of careful risk assessment, it is possible to identify factors that, in collaboration with the service user, our colleagues and other agencies, can be managed so as to minimise the possibility of harm.

It is, however, important to remember that tragic and unfortunate events can, and do, happen. Risk assessment demands the answering of certain key questions. This chapter outlines these questions along with the reasons for asking them, but we are likely to be asking difficult, searching questions of both the service user themselves and others who have known him or her. Despite the plethora of tools, models, forms and policies that have appeared in recent years, risk assessment is far from the simple 'paper exercise' it may first appear. As yet there appears to be no 'industry standard' model of risk assessment in widespread use. 'Tick box' tools and so-called 'risk screening' are prevalent, but can lead to a false sense of security on the part of staff who may be tempted to think that the completion of a brief questionnaire means that a service user has been adequately assessed for the potential harm they may cause to others or themselves (Maden 2007). Risk screen tools have their uses in identifying areas for further focus and information gathering, but are most certainly the beginning, rather than the end, of the mental health risk process.

The use of paper or electronic tools also perpetuates the idea that risk assessment is sometimes perceived as an 'event' or 'task' that is a carried out at a fixed time, often at the start of an agency's contact with a new service user. While initial contact will certainly involve some form of referral, information gathering and usually a meeting with the subject of the referral (see following page) risk assessment can be more accurately described as an ongoing and dynamic process incorporating factors that change constantly with time and circumstance, and will guide the assessment and management of the potential risks posed.

Risk assessment and management does involve recording and documentation, but is above all an opportunity to develop and use communication and rapport-building skills as well as one's own experience and intuition.

First contact

In some (but not all) situations, agencies or individual workers will be required to conduct a formal assessment process based on a referral from a third-party organisation. Examples might include the referral of a hospital patient to a specialist housing provider, or referral of a housing association tenant to day-care services. Risk is not necessarily a concern at this stage, but there are several useful pointers toward a 'good practice' model for staff acquainting themselves with prospective service users.

The referral

A written or verbal referral should contain everything needed in order to offer an individual an appointment for assessment, although they can typically vary in quality from the highly detailed to the bare minimum, such as a name, a date of birth and an address.

The referrer should make clear that they have discussed this with the person concerned, and that they have given consent for their details to be shared with a third party. A 'usable' referral will also include at least a valid reason for the referral (including what it is that the client hopes to achieve with your service), and some background information including any relevant personal history and an account of the person's current mental health problems. The referrer should also draw attention to any current risk behaviours or other immediate concerns.

Assuming that some form of meeting will take place prior to any further action being taken, more information about the individual and their current circumstances may be sought before offering an appointment.

An invitation to meet

A letter or telephone call is likely to be the first contact with the person who has been referred. As well as informing them of the location and time of the appointment, it is important to make them aware of who will be present at the meeting, and why. Some contact details might also be provided should the appointment need to be changed.

The appointment

Most people feel a little uncomfortable meeting strangers, and an assessment interview is likely to be one of the less relaxed situations a prospective client will encounter. For this reason an initial meeting might ideally be carried out with the referrer present, or with someone known to the subject of the assessment. For workers carrying out an assessment interview, it may be helpful to be accompanied by a colleague who can not only supply an alternative viewpoint, but can also share note-taking or recording tasks. When arranging the location of the meeting, the referral information and client's history should aid the decision, particularly with a view to any potential risks that may have been identified. If the person to be interviewed has a history of 'acting out' in stressful situations, we might wish the interview to take place in a safer environment than, for example, a home address.

There are a number of factors to consider when deciding on the time of the appointment. First, how long should the interview last? Consider that a brief ten-minute 'meet and greet' is hardly allowing for the forming of rapport or a detailed assessment of a person's suitability for a service, while a two-hour interview is likely to leave the interviewee (not to mention the assessor) feeling bored, irritable or restless.

We have already highlighted the potential stresses of such a situation, and our first task on meeting a prospective client is to try and put them at ease. If conducting an initial meeting with a colleague, a decision might be made beforehand as to who will 'take the lead' in the assessment, and respective roles should be explained to the interviewee beforehand. Confidentiality policies should be explained, and the subject of assessment reassured that information will be shared only with their consent and on a 'need to know' basis unless issues of public safety are raised.

The worker leading the assessment should check that the individual knows why they have been referred, and then explain the reason and purpose for the assessment. At the start of the assessment, it might also be wise to suggest that they request a break if at any time they feel the need.

If the person to be assessed appears to be under the influence of either drugs or alcohol, there is little likelihood of being able to form a rapport or to obtain a realistic picture of that person. In this instance it should be explained to the person that the assessment meeting will not go ahead, and another appointment made if this seems appropriate.

Identifying risk factors

The identification of risk factors can be thought of initially as a process of information gathering or collation, in particular the key areas of history and background that will best inform our awareness of an individual and the potential risks involved. Obviously, resources may be limited, and some prioritisation may be a useful means of determining the resources devoted to the risk assessment process, although how the combination of degree and likelihood is managed will be determined by each organisation's own policies and procedures.

Without doubt, the key to any good risk assessment process is history and information. A truly thorough risk assessment will demand time, resources and persistence, particularly where service users have arrived with a poorly documented or chaotic history.

The following factors are not exhaustive, but will usually form the key elements of a comprehensive assessment process.

Mental health

It is often assumed (especially by those sceptical of care in the community) that violence and suicide are inextricably linked with mental illness. Statistics tell us this is a considerable misinterpretation. The majority of violent crimes are not committed by people with mental health problems (Friedman 2006). The majority of suicides are committed by people who have had little or no contact with psychiatric services or a general practitioner before their deaths (National Confidential Inquiry 2014).

But some of the individuals we work with will have a history of mental health problems associated with aggression, self-injury or severe neglect. Where the service user has had recent contact with health or social services, a Care Programme Approach care plan (see Infobox: page 76) should be available containing most of the details you will require. If the service user is not known to us, then the first point of contact other than the service user him or herself will be the care co-ordinator or at least someone who has the most up-to-date knowledge of that individual's care.

A history of mental health problems will include at the very least a diagnosis or some description of the individual's experience of mental illness, and how that history has interacted with any risk behaviours. For example, an individual with a history of depression may have attempted suicide in the past, or may have experienced episodes of mania during which they have made themselves vulnerable to sexual exploitation.

The service user will obviously be able to provide the most intuitive information, but at times a precise chronological history may be unavailable from the individual due to cognitive impairment, their mental state, or difficulties understanding and accepting their history of mental illness. Information from third parties such as family, friends or past carers will always be important, and invaluable in circumstances where the service user is unable to provide a clear history. Details of third-party contacts, such as telephone numbers, e-mail addresses and the relationship they have to the service user, should be carefully recorded, particularly as these details may be required should a crisis or change of situation occur. Depending on the nature of this information, consideration should be given to where third-party information is recorded.

Some individuals may have a track record of early warning signs (see page 49), which might precede a deterioration in a person's mental health and any subsequent risk behaviours, and these should be carefully noted in addition to any known adverse reactions to particular events ('trigger factors'), such as anniversaries, contact with certain people, seasons, or simply a lack of cigarettes. If these are known, they need to be clearly recorded.

Written records are an obviously valued source of information, but can be misleading, particularly where assessors have not had the opportunity to meet the individual for themselves. Occasionally, important risk factors may have been either minimised or omitted altogether from written reports.

Medication

The story of the schizophrenic killer who had stopped taking his or her medication before the crime is a media favourite when covering mental health-related homicide. This is almost always a gross over-simplification. Anti-psychotic medication and to a lesser extent mood stabilisers do appear to play a role in moderating acts of violence by seriously mentally ill people (Fazel *et al.* 2014), and statistics for both homicide and suicide in the UK do point to a significant contribution of medication non-adherence to these tragic events. But for mental health workers undertaking risk work, it is more than just a question of whether or not a service user is taking, or not taking, their medication. It is important to understand the relationship between a service user's attitude toward medication, why they may decline to take medication such as anti-psychotics, and what history tells us about the consequences (if any) of non-adherence.

For this reason it is important to determine not only what medications (if any) the person is taking, but what their attitudes and feelings are toward medication, and whether they suffer side-effects from all or any of the drugs they are prescribed. It is surprisingly common for patients to have little or no knowledge of the medications they are prescribed, or to have any idea how they work (Aldridge 2012). Lack of awareness and knowledge of prescribed medications is a key factor in non-adherence (Aldridge 2012; Berk *et al.* 2010) and should therefore form a key part of the risk assessment, and help should be sought from the prescriber (usually either a psychiatrist or GP) or other mental health professional working with the service user. Finally, the person's care plan should also include details of how medication should be administered and/or supervised.

Alcohol and other non-prescribed drugs

The link between substance misuse and mental illness has long been established as an important factor in risk assessment. A number of UK studies have shown that in a country with some of the highest substance misuse rates in the world, people with mental health problems are even more likely than the general population to take drugs or drink heavily. The relationship between violence, suicide and other negative impacts has been amply demonstrated to increase markedly among those who are mentally ill and also use alcohol and/or drugs to a significant level (Crome and Chambers 2009).

Any risk assessment should routinely include an alcohol and drugs history, and where possible should be corroborated by third-party sources. However, assessing an individual's relationship with non-prescribed drugs goes beyond how many cans of beer they drink or joints they smoke in the course of a day. The assessment also needs to determine how the person is affected by the substances they use, and to attempt to find out why they use non-prescribed drugs. Of course, they may reply that they seek the same mix of relaxation, euphoria or simply having a good time as most other people who drink alcohol, snort legal highs or smoke cannabis; but often there are more complex factors involved, and it is important that the assessment attempts to determine the relationship between a service user's mental health, their use or misuse of drugs and any incidents of concern that have been associated with this relationship in the past, or in the present.

Social support and relationships

Factors such as the symptoms or effects of mental illness can inform our assessment of risk, as does the effect of drugs and alcohol on any relevant situations or incidents that have happened in the past and are perhaps likely to happen again in the future. While these are essential elements to the overall assessment, the risks posed by one individual are unlikely to be influenced purely by internal factors such as low mood or, for example, a history of amphetamine abuse, but also by facets of the world around him or her that interact with their internal world to provoke anger, distress or violence.

A personal history is essential to an understanding of a service user's situation. A key part of the assessment is determining what circumstances, events or relationships have been most important to that person, and how these have led them to be here talking to us. Conversation with a mental health care co-ordinator, family, carers or professionals who have known the individual previously will be invaluable, particularly where he or she has difficulty providing an account for themselves. An assessor may need to find out where a person has been living in recent years, and discover a little about their lifestyle, what they do for a living or how they occupy their time. Where key professionals or carers have been involved in the past, it is often a good idea to ask the subject of the assessment for permission to contact that worker for any further contribution they may be able to make in our assessment.

Where the person has been a hospital in-patient during this time, an attempt should be made to speak to a mental health professional who has known them during this time. Even if a discharge summary has been provided, this will not necessarily include all incidents or situations that may have caused concern and may be repeated given a particular set of circumstances.

Some individuals may have lost touch with family, particularly where relationships in early life have been strained or even non-existent, but the assessment will benefit greatly from an exploration of the person's interaction with others, particularly where either past or current relationships have had some bearing on their mental health or, for example, a violent incident. Where family or social relationships are complex and have a direct bearing on the assessment of risk, it might be worth designing a 'genogram' (a diagrammatic representation of family and social relationships) with the service user to highlight particular aspects of their history that may have caused difficulty or led to untoward situations or incidents.

Offending and aggression

It is important to note that risk assessment is a global process involving the identification of factors that may contribute to various forms of undesirable or dangerous events, and while criminal acts form only part of the overall risk profile, a history of offending is universally acknowledged as a key indicator of future offending and is an area that must be researched as part of our overall assessment.

Where service users do have a history of offending it is important to have some form of chronological record of offences, and where gaps exist these should be clearly recorded along with reasons why the service user's offending history is not fully comprehensive. It is not always the case that incidents of assault or aggression result in criminal conviction, particularly where the perpetrator has spent periods of time as a hospital in-patient or in supported accommodation. For this reason it is important that we try to research and record any such incidents, including, for example, attacks on staff or other service users or incidents of sexual harassment or assault. Sometimes even recorded offences will have little bearing on the nature of the incident itself. For example, an incident of fire setting may not always result in a charge of arson but may be downgraded to criminal damage. Sex without consent may be considered as sexual assault rather than rape. While a list of recorded convictions may be of some use, assessments will benefit from a much greater understanding of the context and circumstances of a service user's offending. Where an offending history exists, it is essential that at least some aspect of motives, victims, substance use and any other important factors are identified.

Individuals will often be (unsurprisingly) reluctant to discuss past criminal offences, but where appropriate (see Confidentiality, page 96) information may be sought from professionals who have prior acquaintance with the subject of the assessment.

Finally, it is also important to identify and recognise any existing legal restrictions or court orders (e.g. Antisocial Behaviour Orders, or suspended sentences) that may apply. This may not be divulged by the subject of the order, and may not be immediately obvious, particularly where that person has moved from place to place or has led a chaotic lifestyle with little contact from health or social services workers.

Confidentiality

One of the most frequently asked questions from mental health agencies such as housing providers concerns the question of referrers being unwilling to disclose sensitive information (such as criminal records) about clients. Whether this is born of a genuine concern on the part of the referrer to maintain client confidentiality on the one hand, or a more cynical ploy to successfully accommodate an otherwise 'difficult to place' individual, it is a constantly recurring problem.

The advent of community care has highlighted the issue of information sharing between health, social services and agencies such as providers of housing and day-care services. A lack of communication and a reluctance on the part of referrers to share important information regarding histories of violence and offending has been identified as a key factor in several inquiry reports into serious crimes perpetrated by mentally ill people.

Health and social services professionals are placed in the difficult position of being bound by professional codes of conduct that stress the importance of maintaining patient or client confidentiality, and seeking the express consent of the individual to reveal information about themselves to third parties. Unsurprisingly, those who have a criminal record may be unwilling for this information to be disclosed and may expressly forbid professionals from disclosing this to others.

On the other hand, most health and social care organisations have clearly defined policies and procedures on confidentiality. Most echo the general principle that maintaining confidentiality is paramount while making clear that where information directly concerns issues of public or client safety (e.g. a history of assault or attempted suicide) then these facts warrant disclosure, albeit on a strictly 'need to know' basis. In cases where either referrers or care providers are unsure of whether or not to disclose information, or are concerned that key facts concerning risk have been withheld, it may be possible to seek the advice of a local 'Caldicott Guardian' (see below) for further guidance.

Another key question that often causes confusion is when, or in what circumstances, information should be disclosed to the police. Again, local and organisational policies will mostly dictate good practice in this area, but as a rule of thumb the principle of public and client safety is an overarching guide. Assuming some form of crisis has occurred to warrant police involvement (such as a disappearance or a violent incident), carers might need to disclose whatever information is *essential* for officers to offer support and intervene.

CALDICOTT GUARDIANS

In 1997 the Government appointed Dr Fiona Caldicott to investigate concerns around patient confidentiality raised by emerging methods of electronic record-keeping in health and social care. As a result of Dr Caldicott's report, all National Health Service Trusts and local authority social services departments are now required to appoint a 'Caldicott Guardian' (Department of Health 1999). Caldicott Guardians are senior staff designated to protect patient or client information, and to provide guidance and strategic development (e.g. the design of policies and procedures) around confidentiality. Each organisation's Caldicott Guardian is also responsible for ensuring that legislation, such as the Data Protection Act 1998 and the Mental Health Act 1983, is adhered to by their organisation's working practices.

Managing risk

By the end of the information gathering stage, a large amount of data has been collated that will guide and inform a risk management plan. Whether this is a 'standalone' document or incorporated within a care plan, risk management should ideally be born of collaboration between the worker(s) who carried out the initial assessment, their colleagues, other agencies involved in the care of the service user, and of course the service user him or herself. The regular CPA reviews convened by a service user's care co-ordinator are an ideal forum to discuss risk management with the subject of the plan in a multi-disciplinary environment.

The process of devising a risk management strategy involves the processing of large amounts of information and using the key points to identify and manage key areas of risk. Readers of a culinary bent will be familiar with the process of 'reducing' a sauce, whereby a pan of liquid is slowly simmered until much of the liquid has evaporated and a thicker, more concentrated sauce is left. This is exactly what will happen with the collated information.

The assessment phase may have yielded a large volume of information, particularly in cases where the service user has along history of contact with mental health services and/or other agencies, such as housing providers. Some of this information will prove vital in the management of any identified risks, while some may be interesting, but essentially superfluous to a simple, transparent risk management plan.

Having interviewed the service user, and perhaps read reports and spoken to third parties, the assessor should now have a reasonably good idea of what risk factors exist, and how they interact. This information now needs to be condensed by reviewing the recorded information and picking out key points that will need to be addressed.

The final stage is to look at the risk factors with the service user (if he or she is willing) and devise a strategy for managing risk that takes into account the potential hazards identified, a formulation of how these hazards interact with the person's past and current situation, and a list of actions to minimise the risks along with a clear identification of who is responsible for each action. It may be appropriate for a care plan or risk management strategy to highlight possible 'trigger factors' and offer a profile of early warning signs. A 'crisis plan' might also be required here, particularly if there is an identified likelihood of situations deteriorating over a short period of time. A crisis plan should include details of relevant contacts and clear instructions as to what needs to be done given a particular set of circumstances such as a service user's unexplained disappearance, or the emergence of early warning signs. Finally, the simple mnemonic ORCAS (Ongoing, Reviewed, Communicated and Simple) (see Infobox below) is a useful means of remembering the most important principles of designing and implementing a risk management strategy.

Infobox: ORCAS (Ongoing, Reviewed, Communicated and Simple)

A simple mnemonic to outline the key principles of risk assessment and management.

Ongoing
Risk is a dynamic process and situations will change over time. Risk factors need to be continually monitored.

Reviewed
A risk management strategy warrants regular review involving both the client and all professionals and carers involved in his or her care. If meetings have been arranged, it is a care

co-ordinator's responsibility to invite relevant parties to a meeting at a mutually convenient time at which attendance should be prioritised.

Communicated

Clear lines of communication between colleagues, clients and other key individuals are essential for effective risk management. Numerous inquiry reports have highlighted time after time how poor communication between agencies has led to serious incidents and, in some cases, death.

Simple

A risk management strategy is of little use if it looks like a wiring diagram, or is buried within a pile of notes in a cupboard. As a point of reference, the strategy should be easily comprehensible to anyone involved in the care of the client, from the care co-ordinator to a locum or agency housing worker.

CASENOTES: RISK ASSESSMENT AND MANAGEMENT

Jenny

Jenny is 45 and has a 20-year history of schizophrenia. She is well known by the local CMHT and has been admitted to various hospitals a number of times following relapses of her psychotic illness. For most of her adult life she has slept rough, has drunk heavily and drifted from place to place. She has also engaged in prostitution to fund her drinking, which she claims is a far more effective anti-psychotic than the tablets her psychiatrist prescribes for her. She has been sexually assaulted a number of times, either while drunk or during periods of acute illness when she occasionally strips naked and claims to be an 'Earth Goddess'.

For the past year she has been living in a flat provided by a supported housing organisation, who have allocated a keyworker who visits regularly to collect rent and offer support. She has a very good relationship with the keyworker, and has begun to attend a horticulture course at a local college. Jenny also visits a local Mental Health Day Centre, and has a community psychiatric nurse (who is also her care co-ordinator under the Care Programme Approach) who convenes CPA reviews every six months and helps Jenny come to terms with her diagnosis of schizophrenia, and understand the effects of the anti-psychotic medication she is prescribed.

Jenny has no criminal record and denies ever having been violent toward others, but has tried to kill herself on several occasions over the last 20 years. Prior to moving into her new flat, Jenny had been admitted to hospital after an attempt to kill herself with a large overdose of paracetamol combined with several litres of strong cider. She reports that this was prompted by her becoming upset by beliefs that people were spreading rumours about her, namely that she was having sex with young boys. She was referred to the special needs housing association and discharged to her flat after several months in hospital, during which time she was treated with anti-psychotic medication and helped to learn more about her illness and the effect that alcohol has upon her.

Jenny's life has been remarkably stable for the last year. She has made friends locally, looks after her flat and her illness has been well controlled with medication. She has reduced her alcohol intake considerably although still binge drinks occasionally to cope with difficult life events. Jenny has no contact with family, although she had a baby 20 years ago who was given up for adoption. She has recently had some contact from social services informing her that her son is now trying to trace her and would like to meet her. Jenny remains ambivalent about this.

Mental health: Jenny suffers from schizophrenia and has experienced frequent relapses, which are often brought about by alcohol misuse. She is prescribed anti-psychotic medication, but has in the past failed to take this in the belief that alcohol is more effective in treating her symptoms.

Alcohol and other non-prescribed drugs: Jenny has a long history of alcohol abuse which she uses to 'self-medicate', although alcohol appears to worsen her psychotic symptoms. Has reduced alcohol intake since discharge from hospital, but still binge drinks when stressed.

Social support and relationships: Jenny has no family but is otherwise well supported in the community. Previously she has slept rough and lived a chaotic existence. She has a son who wishes to make contact with her after being adopted as a baby.

Offending and aggression: No history recorded or reported.

Suicide and self-harm: Jenny has made several life-threatening suicide attempts. The last was three months ago by using a large amount of paracetamol tablets combined with alcohol and preceded by paranoid delusional ideas.

Other factors (1): Jenny has been left with quite extensive liver damage through a combination of long-term alcohol abuse and several overdose attempts. She has been warned that a further major overdose will prove almost certainly fatal.

Other factors (2): Jenny is vulnerable to sexual exploitation and assault.

Conclusions: From even a relatively small amount of information a 'formulation' of the risks posed in this case can devised. The risks fall into three main categories:

- suicide

- sexual assault/exploitation

- self-neglect.

It is not possible to make any precise predictions as to whether these risk factors will happen again or not, although the mental health team and the housing providers could minimise the risks by exerting a higher degree of support or even containment. However, Jenny now lives independently and enjoys a better quality of life than she has experienced for many years.

A formulation of Jenny's situation and circumstances suggests some relationship between her mental health problems, alcohol abuse and the identified risk factors, although the exact dynamics of this relationship are still not entirely clear from the information available here. In the short term, a potential 'trigger factor' has been identified in the fact that her son wishes to make contact after being adopted as a baby, a situation with the potential to upset Jenny.

Risk management

After careful consideration and discussion between Jenny, her housing association keyworker and her care co-ordinator, a care plan is produced focusing on managing the substantial risks posed by Jenny to herself. The care plan identifies the potential hazards that may befall Jenny, and makes clear the need to minimise the potential for relapse into psychotic illness by providing ongoing social and professional support, helping Jenny cope with life stresses (such as her son's wish to make contact with her) without recourse to alcohol, and help her maintain compliance with the medication she is prescribed.

Jenny agrees that she will inform one of her care workers immediately should she feel tempted to attempt suicide, and she has consented to her care co-ordinator contacting her horticultural tutor to request that he alerts the CMHT should Jenny not attend as usual or present any cause for concern. Finally, the care co-ordinator will take a detailed look at Jenny's history and work with her to draw up a profile of early warning signs that might be recognised as indicators of her becoming unwell.

Ongoing risk management

The care plan and risk management strategy is constantly revised as circumstances change, and reviewed regularly at CPA meetings by those involved.

Jenny: Points for reflection

1. Jenny prefers to 'self-medicate' with alcohol rather than taking prescribed medication. How does her alcohol abuse contribute to the overall risks involved?

2. Part of Jenny's Risk Management Plan involves identification of early warning signs. Can you suggest examples of what these might be?

3. Of the risk assessment and management factors outlined above, which are the most important in both the short and longer term?

References

Aldridge, M.A. (2012) 'Addressing non-adherence to antipsychotic medication: A harm-reduction approach.' *Journal of Psychiatric and Mental Health Nursing 19,* 1, 85–96.

Berk, L., Hallam, K.T., Colom, F., Vieta, E. *et al.* (2010) 'Enhancing medication adherence in patients with bipolar disorder.' *Human Psychopharmacology: Clinical & Experimental 25,* 1–16.

Crome, I., Chambers, P., Frisher, M., Bloor, R. and Roberts, D. (2009) *The Relationship between Dual Diagnosis: Substance Misuse and Dealing with Mental Health Issues.* London: Social Care Institute for Excellence.

Department of Health (1999) *Health Service Circular 1999/012: Caldicott Guardians.* London: Department of Health.

Fazal, S., Zetterqvist, J., Larsson, H., Långström, N. and Lichtenstein, P. (2014) 'Antipsychotics, mood stabilisers, and risk of violent crime.' *Lancet 384,* 9949, 1206–1214.

Friedman, R.A. (2006) 'Violence and mental illness: How strong is the link?' *New England Journal of Medicine 355,* 2064–2066.

Hughes, K., Bellis, M.A., Jones, L., Woods, S. *et al.* (2012) 'Prevalence and risk of violence against adults with disabilities: A systematic review and meta-analysis of observational studies.' *Lancet 379*, 9826, 1621–1629.

Maden, A. (2007) *Treating Violence A Guide to Risk Management in Mental Health.* Oxford: Oxford University Press.

National Confidential Inquiry (2014) *Annual Report 2014: England, Northern Ireland, Scotland and Wales.* Manchester: University of Manchester.

Ritchie, J., Dick, D. and Lingham, R. (1994) *The Report of the Inquiry into the Care and Treatment of Christopher Clunis.* London: HMSO.

Chapter 4

CHALLENGING BEHAVIOUR

Most of us working in mental health and social care will have encountered service users who are aggressive, threatening or just very 'difficult'. Challenging behaviour has serious short- and longer-term consequences for both service users and those around them. A number of alternative euphemisms have been introduced to avert the castigation of this group, who can behave anti-socially, reject support and are sometimes openly hostile toward our well-intended offers of help.

Whether readers work in residential care, mental health units or community outreach they will encounter a small but highly visible group of service users of all backgrounds and ages who can sometimes behave in ways that are anti-social, aggressive or even dangerous toward both themselves and others. Much of the literature and thinking around challenging behaviour has focused on schoolchildren, learning disability and people on the autistic spectrum, but despite a large volume of research evidence and discussion on the subject of risk, violence and mental illness, very little attention has been paid to the subject of working with challenging individuals within a mental health care context.

This section of the book is not intended to suggest that mentally ill people are aggressive or difficult by default. As

Friedman (2006) points out, 'most people who are violent are not mentally ill and most people who are mentally ill are not violent'. Nonetheless, people who are troubled by distressing perceptions, are angry, or have limited means of communicating will sometimes present problems that are responded to with panic, fright or outright avoidance.

Challenging people are challenging for many different reasons, but are no less deserving of our care and support than anyone else. The real challenge for services is to find ways of responding that are proactive rather than reactive, that are well planned and consistent across the various interventions that service users will be offered, and that are compassionate yet boundaried. This chapter focuses on the longer-term problems of challenging behaviour. Incidents of aggression or threat can occur randomly and sporadically, but most often happen within situations that are associated with a service user over a period of time and can be prepared for to some degree with plans for the assessment and management of risk, and a protocol of response that is predetermined (preferably with the service user) and consistent within a group of workers and perhaps other agencies who work with that person.

To do this we're going to be thinking about challenging behaviour and challenging people in a systematic, thoughtful way. We're going to be using a simple, step-by-step framework called CAPE (see page 112), and collecting a 'Toolkit' of skills and attitudes we either already use, or will develop in time.

We are talking here about working with, not against, challenging behaviour. It is about working as a team, using clear, consistent frameworks and strategies to replace the frustration, panic or avoidance that so often engulfs us when faced with behaviours that are harmful to ourselves, other people, or the service user him or herself.

Face-to-face reactions to challenge and crisis intervention are a somewhat different area that require real-life experience and training as part of a staff group, but we shall outline the essentials of de-escalation and communication skills later in this chapter.

What is 'challenging behaviour'?

One of our first problems is to locate challenging behaviour within a context and setting. In other words, what is seen as challenging in one environment may not be seen as remotely problematic in another. The importance of having a clear local definition of challenging behaviour appropriate to our location and circumstances is emphasised by the first part of our CAPE model: Clarification.

Verbal threats that may be seen as little more than occupational hazard in one setting could be viewed as a serious issue in another. Sexual disinhibition at an elderly care home may be seen as harmless in that environment, but another matter indeed within a secure psychiatric unit. Even physical aggression has different levels of severity and outcome depending on the setting and context.

There are several definitions of challenging behaviour described in the literature that we can use as a starting point for own local version. One of the best known is Emerson's (1995) definition:

> Culturally abnormal behaviour of such an intensity, frequency or duration that the physical safety of the person or others is likely to be placed in serious jeopardy, or behaviour which is likely to seriously limit use of, or result in the person being denied access to, ordinary community facilities.

Most of our groups of social care workers undertaking training in challenging behaviour find the following useful:

Any behaviour which negatively affects both the 'perpetrator' and those around them to a significant and/or frequent degree. (Kinsella 2013)

Asked to list the most typical examples of challenging behaviour, verbal and physical aggression are commonly cited, but other less obvious behaviours can be described as having an equally negative impact on the service user and those around him or her. Threats, manipulation and lying are less dramatic forms of challenging behaviour but no less powerful in the damage they can cause. Some services may see, for example, self-harm as attention seeking or, on the other hand, a form of communication on the part of a service user who has little other means to seek help from professionals. But whichever the setting and whoever the service user, there are certain principles that we consider fundamental to both the CAPE approach and the Toolkit. They look something like this:

- *People are challenging.* Everyone has the potential to be challenging. As social care professionals we may be reasonably proficient at communicating needs and managing emotions, but all of us experience fear, frustration, tiredness or anger at times. Many readers will be familiar with the disinhibiting effects of alcohol. In fact, most of the factors that contribute to the challenging behaviour of service users are no different to those experienced by ourselves at some stage. We are (on the whole, and for a wide variety of reasons) simply better at managing our behaviour.

- *Service users are a priority.* This may appear to be a statement of the obvious. In many respects, it is. But once a 'difficult' service user has become labelled as 'challenging' it is easy for that individual to become marginalised and avoided. In some extreme and highly harrowing cases, the challenging service user can themselves become the victim of harassment and abuse.

There are certainly cases where service users can no longer be offered the services we provide, and difficult decisions regarding mental capacity and safety may need to be made. Some examples of challenging behaviour may need to involve police or safeguarding services. But demonisation is never an option.

- *There is always a reason for challenging behaviour.* We often assume that challenging behaviour occurs randomly, especially where service users are affected by cognitive impairments caused by dementia, learning disability or severe mental illness. But all human behaviour occurs for a reason. Even the most seemingly bizarre and incomprehensible acts have some meaning for the person doing them, and the attempt by supporters and carers to identify why a service user is shouting or damaging property is one of the skilled fundamentals of working with vulnerable people (Skills for Care 2013).

- *We are managing, not curing.* Challenging behaviour is not a diagnosis and we are not aiming to 'cure' the service user. We are simply aiming to reduce the severity and frequency of the target behaviour so that life is better for the service user and people around them. While issues of boundary setting and safety maintenance are a priority in challenging behaviour work, there is little or no evidence that punitive options or restraint are either useful or beneficial interventions. Much of this chapter is focused on how services working together safely and consistently with aggressive or anti-social service users can help quality of life for perpetrators and those around them.

- *There are no magic wands.* Our final assumption is that the advice offered here can offer generic principles of good practice and a guide to using a structured approach. Local conditions, individual characteristics (of both service users and ourselves), resources and restrictions will all govern how challenging behaviours are defined and recognised. These local factors will also determine how well we function both as individuals and as part of a team. And some challenging behaviours will not be amenable to any amount of effort and skill, and will carry on indefinitely while we either learn to work around it or find an alternative setting more suited to that person's needs.

The CAPE model

One of the most common problems for staff faced with difficult and challenging service users is a sense of desperation. Service users who are hostile, threatening or aggressive can be extremely frightening, particularly when the behaviour is directed at ourselves or we are charged with the responsibility for containing that behaviour (see Infobox: Staff and Service Users). CAPE came from a need for learners in training to look at challenging behaviour in a more structured, methodical way than is often the case. We all have a tendency to react instinctively rather than planning proactively. CAPE is a four-stage process and stands for Clarification, Assessment, Planning and Evaluation.

Infobox: Staff and Service Users

Care workers are at a relatively high risk of assault compared with other occupational groups. Twenty per cent of all UK employees signed off sick following work-related assaults are employed in social care, despite the latter making up only 5 per cent of the total workforce (Lombard 2010). Unsurprisingly,

---

workers who spend the most time in face-to-face contact with service users experience the highest number of assaults (Anderson and West 2011).

The issue of assaults on staff has been much researched within psychiatric hospital staff, but less so in more community-oriented settings. Nonetheless there are findings that apply to a wider remit of situations. Positive and respectful staff attitudes along with skilled communication have been found in numerous investigations to reduce incidents of aggression and violence by service users (Bowers *et al.* 2011). This probably confirms what most of us would suspect, but this doesn't stop there being numerous examples of very poor attitudes and communication on the part of workers dealing with potentially aggressive people.

In one study psychiatric in-patients perceived environmental conditions and poor communication to be a significant precursor of aggressive behaviour. Nurses, in comparison, viewed the patients' mental illnesses to be the main reason for aggression, although the negative impact of the in-patient environment was recognised (Duxbury and Whittington 2005). A failure to empathise with the experience of the distressed individual, often experiencing frightening phenomena of psychotic illness, has been observed by both authors to be a leading cause of challenging incidents.

'C' for Clarifying

We have already seen how challenging behaviour can have quite different definitions according to location and context. A shared living project for young people may have a very different meaning of challenging behaviour from a residential care home for people with dementia. Even within an individual service, our risk assessment and management plans may suggest different thresholds for individual service users (see Chapter 3).

Within our CAPE approach, Clarification is the first stage of determining how we go on to plan strategies for working with challenging behaviour. This is where we ask the questions: (a) 'What is the behaviour?' and (b) 'Is the behaviour challenging within the definition and context we have defined as a service?' Whether we are *in situ* with a service user or discussing in a training room, we often make the mistake of 'jumping ahead' of ourselves – ascribing meaning and mitigation to a person's verbal threats or destruction of property before starting at the beginning with these questions. We need to be careful here to actually describe the behaviour, and not the emotion behind it. For example, a remark to a female keyworker about the size of her breasts may be passed off as a harmless expression of sexuality from George, an elderly care home resident who is feeling 'a bit frustrated'. But is this a behaviour that would be deemed acceptable in everyday life? Might the remark be deemed deeply offensive by another woman and a potential cause of harm to the service user? The probable answers in this scenario are 'no' and 'yes', but a potential pitfall here is to ascribe age and sexual frustration as a cause of the remark. Clarification is about clearly describing the behaviour with objectivity and, as the name suggests, clarity. We can begin ascribing meaning and cause of challenging behaviour in our Assessment stage.

We also need to be aware of the possibility that an incident we are trying to describe may become the subject of further investigation, for example by the police or by a safeguarding vulnerable adults panel. In this case, detail and clarity is essential.

A key factor in determining where we go next is the clarification of whether a behaviour meets a stated definition of challenging behaviour. We have defined challenging behaviour above, but local circumstances and environment will be key in determining what is significant or frequent enough to warrant further assessment and perhaps an action plan.

'A' for Assessing

The first stage of our framework has asked whether a particular behaviour can be defined as 'challenging' and directs us toward providing a clear, unambiguous description. The Assessment stage is our attempt to look at why challenging behaviour has happened. These are questions best addressed collaboratively with the perpetrator in the aftermath of an incident or certainly at a quieter time, and should certainly be discussed with colleagues within our own service and with other agencies if involved.

One common pitfall is to 'mitigate' for the challenging behaviour before we have actually tried to assess why what happened has happened. In other words, to use our previous example, we ascribe George's sexual inappropriateness to his age, his cultural background and his personality. Staff describe him as 'a bit of a rogue'. What may have caused great offence to a female member of staff could be passed off as the risqué banter of a lively personality. This is not an objective or useful assessment.

This is also the stage where we need to identify our own and our colleagues' role in challenging behaviour. If this seems a surprising statement, think of occasions where an insensitive remark or poor communication skills on our part as workers has worsened or even created a situation that may not have occurred with more skilled, careful intervention. Assuming our Clarification has identified challenging behaviour as genuinely 'challenging', there are many, many questions we can ask at this stage, depending on the context and setting of the behaviour.

Some staff groups like to think in terms of internal (mental illness pathology, motivations, frustrations, beliefs, attitudes, etc.) and external factors such as conflict with others or protection of self from perceived threats. But however we go about Assessing, these are some of the key questions we might ask when trying to determine why challenging behaviour has taken place:

- What is the frequency of the behaviour? Is this a standalone event or one of a series of incidents?

- What is the impact of the behaviour on the person doing it, and on others including staff? Or in other words, who were the victims of the behaviour and how are they affected?

- Is there a pattern of behaviour? In residential care, for example, mealtimes are often a flashpoint for confrontation. Tenants may react angrily (and predictably) to being asked for their rent, or being confronted about tenancy agreements. Over a longer period of time, seasonal changes may be important or incidents may be seen to occur at a particular time of day. Changes in the frequency and severity of challenging behaviour may also tell us a great deal about an individual's mental state, or might communicate a degree of distress that might not be otherwise evident.

- Is there an antecedent for a person's behaviour other than those we have already mentioned? Behaviour almost never occurs purely at random regardless of the cognitive or functional abilities of the perpetrator.

- What are the consequences for the service user? Challenging behaviours are often well-practised actions that have served the perpetrator well for many years. Perhaps an angry outburst here or a threat of violence there helps that man or woman regain some control over a life that has been lived for the most part in institutions of one form or another. Communication (confused by some with 'attention seeking') may also be a key reward for an act of aggression or destructive anger.

- Are drugs and/or alcohol an antecedent of challenging behaviour? Most of us are more than familiar with the association between intoxication and self-destructive or anti-social behaviour, but where amphetamines, legal highs, super-strength lager or a combination of multiple substances are associated with aggression or threatening behaviour we also need to try and discover how and why drugs and alcohol affects behaviour. An assessment that simply states 'Sharon gets angry when she is drunk and then smashes things' may be factually correct but is a little too light on detail to be genuinely useful to either Sharon or ourselves.

The above is just a small selection of areas we might want to examine during our Assessment, but our most useful tool is our own knowledge and rapport with the people with whom we work. The best informant of all is of course the person presenting the challenging behaviour. It is surprising how often the most obvious question of all – 'Why did you do it?' – hasn't been asked.

'P' for Planning

This is our 'doing' or 'intervention' stage, which will be informed by our Clarification and Assessment process. Different services use different terminology to mean the same thing, but all statutory and non-statutory services have an 'action plan', 'care plan' or 'support plan' that clearly states what we and service users are hoping to achieve, and how we are to go about achieving those goals. No attempt at promoting long-term positive behaviours with clients can be made without a care plan. Even in its simplest form, the care plan is a clearly written account of a client's needs (including the need to behave in a more socially acceptable manner), assessment and set of instructions to be universally followed by both the client and those working with them.

One of our initial assumptions is that we are not trying to eradicate or 'cure' a pattern of anti-social, destructive behaviours. We are attempting to work with the service user to reduce the frequency of challenging behaviours, or at least to reduce their impact on others, ourselves and the service user him or herself.

Whether we are in constant contact with service users in, for example, residential or hospital care, or have a more fleeting relationship as outreach workers, our challenging behaviour assessment should have informed us of what it is that the service user gains from what they do, which in turn informs what it is that may need to change. Changes may be as simple as altering some aspect of the environment (e.g. separating two residents who frequently come into conflict) or working with a service user to suggest alternative ways of dealing with their neighbours. Some readers may be involved in behaviour modification plans with service users, but most encouragement toward more positive behaviours is of a smaller scale with easily achievable goals and clear, unambiguous ideas.

There are some useful points we might try to remember when focusing our plans on the management of challenging behaviour:

- *Realism.* We shall see later in the Toolkit section the importance of pragmatism in working with difficult and sometimes deeply ingrained behaviours (page 123). Care plans that attempt to set unrealistic goals may make failure inevitable and place further pressure on carers, workers and the client themselves. Where goals are set, care plans will also need to indicate some form of measure to indicate whether that goal has been met when reviewed. For example, a client who is constantly irritable and abusive may be set a target to be entirely 'pleasant and co-operative' until the next review in three months' time. This is a prime example of 'setting up the service user to fail'.

First, there needs to be some objective measure of what 'pleasant and co-operative' actually means, and even in the unlikely event that this could be easily defined, the time period (three months) is unrealistically long! The care plan's goals may be more effective by defining more easily identifiable objectives (to both ourselves and the client him or herself) that are limited to a shorter time period and therefore rendered far more achievable.

- *Boundary setting.* Care plans or action plans often fail where there is inconsistency within a staff group. One individual, or set of individuals may set very different boundaries from others, or indeed not set them at all. It is important that boundaries are known and set by all members of staff as well as the service user and his or her family.

  In some cases it may be necessary and/or useful to set clear parameters beyond which a service user's behaviour triggers police involvement, or at least a review of placement or tenancy. It has been known for even serious assaults or incidents to be 'mitigated' by workers so that situations (such as assault, arson or serious criminal damage) that could and should be police matters are managed internally without clear, functional clarification or assessment, and a staff group's dismissal of the behaviour as a result of hearing voices or frustration at having run out of cigarettes. Training room experience with many hundreds of social care workers in similar situations suggests that assumption of police lack of interest in incidents involving mentally ill people presents a barrier to requesting their involvement.

  There is certainly a good argument for not treating mentally ill service users to quite the same expectations and parameters as anyone else. Alternatively, a cursory use of online search engines will reveal many social care examples of inappropriate tolerance to anti-social behaviour that have ended in tragedy. Clear parameters, boundaries and thresholds that are consistent and well understood by staff and service users may prove a highly worthy addition to a service user's plan, as is the ability to sometimes step back and see challenging behaviour for how it might appear if it happened outside the support environment and wasn't subject to the assumptions that we sometimes make about people with mental health problems.

- *Early warning signs.* Staff who know their clients well are usually well aware of certain indicators that are a clear warning of future problems. These often take the form of changes of behaviour, or quite subtle non-verbal cues (such as facial expression), which only those who know the person well may be able to identify as a precursor of challenging behaviours to come. A care plan can benefit immensely from the identification of early warning signs, and the inclusion of key interventions that have been found to help the service user avert problem behaviours before they begin.

- *Trigger factors.* Trigger factors are simply those particular stimuli that previous experience has shown may increase the risk of the service user becoming anxious or angry or feeling threatened. It might be worth reminding ourselves here that challenging behaviours almost always arise from the emotions and feelings of the perpetrator, not the perpetrator themselves. Trigger factors are again best identified by those who know the person well, and can take the shape of anything from certain television programmes to particular dates or seeing somebody wearing clothing of a particular colour.

'E' for Evaluating

By now we have (hopefully) concluded that a consensual, structured, proactive approach to challenging behaviour is more likely to achieve our outcomes than staff responses that are haphazard, reactive and fuelled by panic, fear or resignation. As pointed out above, there is always the potential for staff who work regularly with challenging behaviours to become 'over sensitised' to verbal or physical aggression, destruction of property or any other of the challenging behaviours we have identified and set out to manage.

Evaluation is a means of at least trying to ensure that we see worrying or dangerous behaviour for what it is; and whether we are constantly evaluating informally with colleagues and service users, or more formally through meetings and reviews, our intention is to review the outcomes of our plan in terms of impact, frequency and quality of life. Regular evaluation adds objectivity to our assessments and plans both in the short and longer terms.

In the shorter term, post-incident review involving staff and service users is a useful learning tool for both. Thinking of review in terms of ABC (antecedents, behaviour, consequences) is another popular and simple means of thinking about incidents of challenging behaviour in a way that, as we have seen throughout this chapter, is step-wise and methodical rather than reactive and instinctive.

The Challenging Behaviour Toolkit

The Toolkit is a collection of simple roles and techniques designed to focus attention on helpful skills and ideas for working with challenging behaviours. These are hopefully factors that we can recognise in ourselves from our day-to-day practice, so are not something new, and that allow us to recognise some of the important skills and interventions we already practise. It is not a definitive list, and many of the tools will, in practice, overlap with one another, but the Toolkit has been found by many workers to be an extremely useful and 'do-able' way of addressing difficult clients and situations.

The Analyst

As has been stressed in this chapter, people do not behave in anti-social or antagonistic ways without there being an underlying reason. The Analyst tries to understand challenging behaviour by trying to understand how it might feel to be in that individual's position, and looking beyond the details of the behaviour to look at and work with the service user on possible causes and precipitating factors.

The Telepath

Much challenging behaviour involves a service user's attempts to communicate with the outside world. For a variety of reasons, people with mental health problems may face difficulties communicating in more 'normal', socially acceptable ways. Aggression and destruction may be means of communicating the fear, anger or despair that cannot be adequately verbalised in the same way as most others.

The Telepath can see beyond the usual professional reactions to bad behaviour and respond in ways that work with the service user, not against.

The Straight Bat

The Straight Bat is simply about being honest and straightforward with service users. This is especially important for people who may have learnt to achieve goals by manipulating others or lying. The Straight Bat presents service users with clear responses to their behaviours, clear options and terminologies that are transparent and difficult to misinterpret or 'bend'. There are often occasions when clients may actually find it helpful to know just how powerfully their attitudes and behaviour affect other people. The Straight Bat is a non-judgemental but robust stance to behaviours that may harm both the service user and those around them.

The Pragmatist

The Pragmatist is able to be realistic as to what can be achieved. Neither Alzheimer's disease nor autism *cause* challenging behaviour. Nonetheless, long-term or degenerative conditions such as these can pose considerable barriers to an individual's ability to learn from experience or appreciate the upset they may cause to others. It is at the Planning stage of our CAPE model where the setting of realistic goals and targets will most benefit from the balance of optimism and realism brought to service users by the Pragmatist.

The Communicator

Many problems that arise between clients and staff are down to poor communication. In fact, poor staff communicators are much more likely to be the victims of assault or threats. Other characteristics identified by both service users and mental health professionals include attitude, lack of understanding, being opinionated, controlling, eager or shy; and attitudes including rudeness, sarcasm, belittling, ignoring and arguing (Bond and Brimblecombe 2004).

The Communicator is an empathic individual who is able to think carefully about how others may see the world around them, and adjusts their behaviour and approach accordingly. The Communicator can appreciate how it feels to be distressed or angry, and while not condoning behaviours that have the potential to be extremely damaging or upsetting to others, can communicate with them in a way that takes account of factors such as sensory impairment or alcohol abuse. The (skilled) Communicator has a huge part to play in successful working with challenging people and situations, and we detail some of the key verbal and non-verbal factors below.

Skilled communication

Verbal skills

ACKNOWLEDGEMENT

This is about letting the service user know they are being heard and understood. We can demonstrate acknowledgement by listening carefully to what is being said and reflecting back key words and phrases to the service user, even where they are distressed or angry. Whether workers or care staff should pursue communication with an individual who is hostile and aggressive is a matter of local policy and risk assessment, but genuine concerns and valid arguments may sometimes be lost by an inability to acknowledge what a service user is trying to say.

SIMPLICITY

Angry people, or those whose cognition and senses are impaired by drugs or alcohol, are unable to process complex information. Simple words, short sentences and keeping to very clear messages may prove invaluable.

It is also advisable to keep dialogue with an angry or distressed person to one member of staff. Attempting to engage with one person not many, and perhaps with a person the service user has rapport with will always carry a greater chance of successful resolution.

LIMIT SETTING

This is about stating clearly and simply what is acceptable and what is not acceptable. If an angry or abusive service user continues to, for example, swear or use threats, we might consider refusing to continue the conversation until they stop. This approach can be effective even where the angry or abusive person is confused or cognitively impaired, and should be applied universally by those involved with the person's care.

Non-verbal skills
TONE OF VOICE

The effective communicator is aware of how they may come across to others, particularly those clients who may have sensory or cognitive impairments. A harsh, loud or condescending tone of voice is perhaps more likely than anything else to result in lack of co-operation or even aggression.

POSTURE

Again, effective non-verbal communication is very much influenced by a worker's own self-awareness in knowing how they come across to others. Standing over a client while they are sitting might be seen as potentially threatening and increase the person's anxiety. A relaxed posture when communicating with a distressed or angry person may yield a greater chance of resolution than a tense, defensive posture.

STILLNESS

Gesticulation and sudden body movements may communicate aggression to an already highly aroused person. What may seem quite normal and part of our usual communication style may be perceived as aggressive and excitable to a person who is less able to understand the communication of others.

PERSONAL SPACE

Different social groups (including age groups) have quite different 'rules' on personal space. Some individuals will be more comfortable with physical proximity than others, and in some situations a client may feel unintentionally threatened and uncomfortable by the physical closeness of a member of staff, particularly someone they do not know well.

Working with some client groups may often involve very close physical proximity and contact, particularly where the person is too disabled or cognitively impaired to attend to their own self-care needs, and while the use of touch can be a very effective means of non-verbal communication, physical contact and proximity can sometimes be a cause of friction, particularly where such interactions are clumsy or carried out without thought.

CASENOTES: CHALLENGING BEHAVIOUR
Miranda

Miranda is 27 years old. She has lived at Maple Lodge (a supported housing scheme for vulnerable women) for two years. She was brought up in several children's homes and foster care, never settling long enough to warrant full-time adoption. She has displayed severe behavioural disturbances since the age of ten, and has spent time in prison for assault, theft and drug-dealing convictions. In the past Miranda has been assessed as a psychiatric in-patient, and has been diagnosed as having borderline personality disorder (BPD) and a mild learning disability.

She is assigned a care co-ordinator from the Community Mental Health Team (CMHT) and has a care plan that proposes avoidance of further in-patient admissions unless absolutely necessary. The care plan and tenancy agreements contain clear policies for dealing with challenging behaviour. Miranda knows that assault and/or criminal damage will result in police involvement, a policy that has been agreed by her Maple Lodge keyworker, the care co-ordinator and the neighbourhood police officer.

Miranda responds poorly to stress, and has previously 'acted out' her frustrations by damaging property and threatening those around her. More recently she has resorted to verbal abuse and implied threats rather than physical aggression, and has a tendency to push boundaries and 'play off' other residents against each other, creating tensions within the resident group.

Miranda has a supportive relationship with Sue, her care co-ordinator from the CMHT, and her Maple Lodge keyworker Helen. The last few months have been relatively problem-free for Miranda, although some of the staff continue to be distrustful of her and feel that her recent progress is little more than 'the calm before the storm'. She attends a dialectical behaviour therapy group for people with BPD, and has gradually become more reliable in attending appointments, taking an active part in house tasks and management. There have been two incidents of concern within the last six months. On both occasions she has come into the house late at night shouting at residents and staff, threatening to 'burn this f****** place down' and smashing property in her room. Both incidents were apparently preceded by binges of strong cider and legal highs shared with a gang of boys at a local park.

She enjoys social media and using her tablet, and has been helped by Sue and Helen to apply for a college course in web design, which she is due to begin at the start of the next academic year. However, with memories still fresh of previous incidents of Miranda's violence and threats, many of which were focused on several staff members in particular, some staff believe this is a step too far and too soon, and have tried to dissuade her from applying. They suggest she will be setting herself up to fail and that attending the course will be a disaster.

As the start of the new term approaches, Miranda becomes increasingly irritable and preoccupied, and has angrily accused both Sue and Helen of not supporting her against the members of Maple Lodge staff who are not fully behind her application for the course. She has also started to warn other residents to be wary of the manager of Maple Road, whom she claims is a 'pervy lesbian' who has made sexual advances to her. She has also accused Beth, a resident with whom she is usually friendly, of stealing an MP3 player lent to her by Helen. Miranda states that if the situation isn't resolved she will 'cut up' Beth with a broken bottle.

Miranda: Points for reflection

1. With reference to the CAPE model, can we:

   a. Clarify whether Miranda is presenting challenging behaviour, and define the behaviour succinctly?

   b. Assess why Miranda is behaving in a challenging way?

   c. Plan how we, as a multi-agency team, might apply the current care plan and make alterations to it as necessary?

   d. Discuss how Miranda's progress (or lack of) can be evaluated?

2. Is Miranda vulnerable?

3. Should the police be involved at this stage?

References ─────────────────────────────

Anderson, A. and West, S.G. (2011) 'Violence against mental health professionals: When the treater becomes the victim.' *Innovations in Clinical Neuroscience 8*, 3, 34–39.

Bond, K. and Brimblecombe, N. (2004) 'Violent incidents and staff views.' *Mental Health Nursing 23*, 6, 10–12.

Bowers, L., Stewart, D., Papadopoulos, C., Dack, C. *et al.* (2011) *Inpatient Violence and Aggression: A Literature Review.* London: Institute of Psychiatry. Available at www.kcl.ac.uk/ioppn/depts/hspr/research/ciemh/mhn/projects/litreview/litrevagg.pdf.

Duxbury, J. and Whittington, R. (2005) 'Causes and management of patient aggression and violence: Staff and patient perspectives.' *Journal of Advanced Nursing 50*, 5, 469–478.

Emerson, E. (1995) *Challenging Behaviour: Analysis and Intervention in People with Learning Difficulties.* Cambridge: Cambridge University Press.

Friedman, R.A. (2006) 'Violence and mental illness: How strong is the link?' *New England Journal of Medicine 355*, 2064–2066.

Kinsella, C. (2013) *Working with Challenging Behaviour: Course Book.* JCK Training.

Lombard, D. (2010) 'Social care staff run high risk of assault.' *Community Care* 19.11.10.

Skills for Care (2013) *Supporting Staff Working with People Who Challenge Services.* Leeds: Skills for Care.

Chapter 5

INTRODUCING PERSONALITY DISORDER

Personality disorder is not an illness or disease, but a condition that results in abnormal ways of thinking, feeling and behaving, which puts people at odds with those around them. Personality disorder does not have 'symptoms' but does have clearly observable effects that are deeply problematic for both themselves and those around them.

Studies have shown personality disorder to be surprisingly common in the general population. The most recent international population studies across 13 countries suggest that around 6 per cent of people worldwide can be said to have a personality disorder (Huang *et al.* 2009). It is highly unlikely that most of this population will have come to the attention of mental health services unless diagnosed with another mental disorder such as depression or schizophrenia. People do not tend to approach their GPs or psychiatrists complaining of anti-social behaviour or difficulties empathising with others. They will be more likely to be living in chaotic, marginal circumstances, perhaps with a history of imprisonment, substance misuse, self-harm and violence to others. But for some of this personality-disordered group, financial, business or political success will come to them as a direct result of their ruthlessness and egocentricity. This is a disorder with a variety of different faces, and is a powerful and potentially harmful label. For this reason psychiatrists are still taught the importance of the Three Ps. In other words, is the disorder Problematic, Persistent and Pervasive enough to warrant a psychiatric diagnosis?

Personality disorder has been shown to be particularly prevalent among certain groups. Studies among clients of drug and alcohol dependency services (Bowden-Jones *et al.* 2004), and the numerous surveys of both male and female prisoner populations (National Collaborating Centre for Mental Health 2013) suggest that substantial proportions of both these groups meet the diagnostic criteria. However, widespread and complex patterns of both personality disorder and other mental health problems in these groups often serve to create a somewhat chaotic scenario in which any strictly medical diagnosis, particularly one as difficult to recognise as personality disorder, remains largely invisible against a backdrop of crisis and catastrophic life events, making recognition and access to treatment yet more difficult.

Regardless of whether personality disorder becomes a medical problem, is part of a person's everyday life, or leads to imprisonment or substance dependence, it is invariably associated with failed and fractured relationships, difficulty forming close bonds with others and the potential to create considerable distress to both the affected individual and those around them.

Despite the pessimism that often surrounds this condition, there is increasing evidence that a number of options for the care, support and treatment of this client group can prove helpful and effective in a variety of settings (Bolton *et al.* 2014; Craissati *et al.* 2011; National Institute for Mental Health in England 2003). This chapter will look at some of the most common features of personality disorder, and suggest some useful ways of working with people who present services with some of their most difficult challenges.

What is personality disorder?

Clear signs of impending personality disorder will frequently have been evident since childhood, often associated with a history of neglect and trauma in early life. Personality disorder has a gradual onset and is persistent throughout the person's life. In other words, it does not 'appear' in adulthood in the same way as bipolar disorder or schizophrenia.

Whereas most forms of mental illness can now be associated with malfunctioning brain receptors and neurotransmitters, researchers have yet to determine any such organic origins for personality disorder. There is certainly no such thing as an 'anti-personality disorder' drug.

Personality disorder is usually associated with deviant, anti-social or aggressive behaviour, often resulting in crisis, hospital admissions or imprisonment. However, it has also been suggested that a number of successful people from politicians, world leaders and business people to actors, rock stars and artists have an otherwise undiagnosed personality disorder, and that the characteristics of an unstable and volatile personality that might otherwise have led to catastrophe have contributed to success, notoriety or both (Babiak and Hare 2007; Ronson 2012).

Nonetheless, for the majority of mental health workers personality disorder means a range of behaviours that invariably present challenges and difficulties to staff, other clients and the individual themselves. There are several different profiles of personality disorder, which often overlap with one another (see page 139), but manipulation of others, aggressive and threatening behaviour, unreliability and challenges to perceived authority and the testing of rules and boundaries are all common features.

Personality-disordered individuals have little ability to control impulses, with a low frustration tolerance and a tendency toward bouts of substance abuse or self-harm. They are inclined toward 'all or nothing' thinking, whereby people or situations are seen as either very good or very bad, with little room for 'in betweens', and tend to be highly 'egocentric' with little or no thought for the needs or feelings of others. They often fail to learn by experience and continue to make the same mistakes over and over again, even when their actions lead to untoward circumstances or personal hardship. Unsurprisingly, people with personality disorder are seldom popular with others and tend to have few genuine friends or close bonds with others. While they can often be superficially charming and humorous, relationships are more likely to be based on instrumental gain rather than the warmth or affection upon which most people would base personal friendships and romantic attachments. Personality disorder has been described in one form or another for several thousand years in a variety of cultures. Pioneers of psychiatry such as Philipe Pinel were writing about *manie sans délire* (insanity without delusion) from the early 19th century onwards, and while the diagnosis has undergone numerous rebrands, descriptions and definitions over the last two hundred years, personality disorder is now clearly defined and categorised into sub-types by both the DSM-5 and ICD-10 classification systems.

Research into the causes of personality disorder has yet to reveal a clear-cut 'aetiology' for the condition. Most mental health staff who have worked with personality-disordered people will be familiar with histories of erratic parenting, childhood trauma and neglect. But growing up within a dysfunctional or abusive background is too simplistic an explanation, and does not explain why siblings from the same family, with similar if not identical backgrounds, often follow very different paths into adulthood, with perhaps one brother or sister developing personality disorder in adulthood while others go on to lead reasonably normal, happy lives. Where one or both parents have shown signs of personality disorder themselves, the question arises as to the relative impact of genetic heredity on their children. In the absence of large-scale twin studies, it is difficult (if not impossible) to separate out the influence of genetic heredity from harsh environmental factors in the development of personality disorder.

A further research complication is the heterogeneity of the disorder, or in other words, the high degree of overlap that exists between one type of personality disorder and another. To further complicate matters, other mental disorders (including, in many cases, dependence on drugs or alcohol) often exist 'comorbidly' with personality disorder.

While the relative importance of childhood development and upbringing is undisputed, the contribution of genetic and organic factors is emerging as an increasingly important area of research. A recent study among young children has highlighted the important role of genetic heredity in the development of some traits associated with future personality disorder, while other anti-social traits were found to have been influenced more by their developmental environment than genes alone (Viding 2013).

Infobox: PD or not PD?

Even the most experienced mental health professionals have great difficulty agreeing with each other on the diagnosis of personality disorder, although both DSM-5 and ICD-10 offer reasonably straightforward definitions. For example, DSM-5 defines personality disorder as:

> An enduring pattern of inner experience and behavior that deviates markedly from the expectations of the individual's culture, is pervasive and inflexible, has an onset in adolescence or early adulthood, is stable over time, and leads to distress or impairment. (American Psychiatric Association 2013)

The standardised criteria by which doctors diagnose illnesses are useful when trying to identify appendicitis, but applying a medical label to the vagaries of human behaviour is an altogether more complex process. Unlike mental illnesses, which are recognised and treated in much the same way throughout the developed world, the diagnosis of personality disorder depends to a large part on a deviation from social and cultural norms which change from one population to the next. What might be seen as anti-social and destructive behaviour in a rural community may merit little more than a shrug of the shoulders in a deprived inner-city community. An otherwise 'normal' social interaction on the streets of London may be seen as grossly offensive in Japan.

Furthermore, the recognised criteria for personality disorder would apply to most of us at various times and within different contexts, although diagnosis depends on personality traits and behaviours being reported *consistently* over a period of time and causing the individual (and those around them) significant problems in their day-to-day lives.

Both classification systems sub-divide personality disorder into a number of categories such as 'histrionic', 'anti-social' or 'narcissistic', but these are largely regarded as unwieldy and difficult to validate as few clinicians are able to agree a 'clean' differentiation between one category and another due to the widely overlapping nature of the personality traits accredited to each diagnostic label.

DSM-5 does offer a relatively useful 'cluster' system, which represents a reasonably accessible means of understanding how clinicians diagnose and study personality disorder and how the condition actually manifests to both the sufferer and those around them. But how do these textbook definitions of personality disorder actually relate to those individuals seen by mental health workers in day-to-day practice, and why is this such an unpopular and controversial diagnosis?

A large proportion of those who meet the diagnostic criteria will never be aware that they have a personality disorder and will never come into contact with a mental health professional, although they may come into contact with the police or draw attention to themselves within their local community. However, they will certainly be more likely than most to have what mental health professionals call a 'comorbid' mental disorder, such as substance dependence or a psychotic illness (Weaver *et al.* 2003), and those that engage in persistently self-destructive or anti-social behaviours (the so-called 'Cluster B' individuals) are more likely to come to the attention of mental health services, supported housing and other care agencies.

A diagnosis of exclusion?

With attributes such as those described earlier, and the fact that personality disorder is often combined with other 'comorbid' mental health problems, such as substance dependence or depression, it is unsurprising that this is such an unpopular condition with both community workers and mental health professionals. The personality-disordered are a population often excluded by services on the grounds that they tend to exhaust both individual workers and the teams with which they work. The effectiveness of hospital in-patient treatment is seen as debatable at best, with only crisis intervention or treatment of comorbid symptoms such as low mood or anxiety being offered as a realistic option by most acute in-patient units, and personality-disordered patients often demanding staff resources grossly out of proportion to their numerical presence. Special hospitals and secure units specialising in the treatment of violent and offender patients provide care for a significant number of personality-disordered individuals. Although most of this group will be detained under the Mental Health Act (see Chapter 7) there remains considerable disparity between individual services as to the treatability or otherwise of personality-disordered patients (National Collaborating Centre for Mental Health 2013).

Of the treatment interventions indicated for personality disorder (see page 142) several are seeing evidence for optimism (NICE 2009a, 2009b). Psychological therapies are also heavily dependent on the full co-operation of the client, which is often not the case even when resources have been identified and referrals made. However, this does not mean that positive outcomes cannot be achieved, particularly within community environments and longer-term placements such as supported housing, where for many individuals stability and relationship-building will begin to replace chaos and isolation, in many cases for the first time in an eventful and turbulent life.

What's in a name?

The recognised disease classification systems break down mental disorder into an occasionally bewildering array of categories and sub-types. The current International Classification of Diseases (ICD-10: World Health Organization 1992) suggests nine separate types of personality disorder, although its 'F60.8 Other specific personality disorders' category includes a further six sub-categories! On the other hand, the DSM-5 (American Psychiatric Association 2013) lists ten separate categories. The component parts of these classification systems are rarely used in practice as the personality traits and behaviours of each category invariably overlap with one another. However, DSM-5 provides a solution to this problem by grouping the sub-categories of personality disorder into three broad 'clusters', which are widely used both in day-to-day practice and research. Some (but not all) of the more frequently observed types of personality disorder are outlined here. Seeing the different types in this context may go some way to explaining why only *some* categories come to the attention of mental health services, while others may have a significant impact on a person's life without necessarily attracting the attention of mental health or other support services.

Cluster A: The 'odd' or 'eccentric' types

Cluster A includes the paranoid, schizoid and schizotypal personality disorders. People with Cluster A disorders are suspicious or even paranoid toward others, and have great difficulty forming relationships with other people, or may even avoid all human contact altogether. Their daily routine and lifestyle is aimed at avoidance of social situations or particular people seen as presenting a potential threat, and tend not to come to local attention, or are simply described by neighbours as 'odd', 'eccentric' or 'weird'.

Although it is relatively unusual for Cluster A personality disorder to be seen in psychiatric clinics or in-patient units, clinicians are careful to make a distinction between personality disorder on the one hand, and a psychotic illness such as schizophrenia on the other. While terms such as 'paranoid' and 'schizoid' suggest a close similarity with severe mental illnesses such as schizophrenia, Cluster A disorders are not *psychotic* disorders. Distrust and suspicion in this context are personality traits as opposed to symptoms of mental illness and will not usually respond to treatment with anti-psychotic drugs, a particularly important distinction where issues of drug treatment or detention under the Mental Health Act are under consideration.

Cluster B: the 'dramatic', 'emotional' or 'erratic' types

This cluster includes the histrionic, narcissistic, anti-social and borderline personality disorders, and is perhaps the most familiar to those working in mental health. Borderline and anti-social personality disorder will be particularly familiar to care staff, and warrant more detailed individual discussion.

Borderline personality disorder (BPD) is characterised by impulsivity, unstable personal relationships and poor self-esteem. People with BPD are often highly ambivalent in their feelings toward others, veering from positive to negative opinions about others while being fearful of abandonment, which they will go to considerable lengths to avoid. Another frequently described feeling is a sensation of 'emptiness' and lack of emotions of any kind.

People with BPD are also highly susceptible to stress, and may react strongly and sometimes dramatically to situations that would not trouble most people. They are prone to self-harm, or sometimes threaten to commit suicide, particularly when they feel rejected or believe that relationships (whether personal or professional) are about to end. As with other forms of personality disorder, BPD is often associated with other mental disorders such as depression or psychosis, and under particular duress the person may become abnormally suspicious or paranoid. BPD is often seen as an essentially 'female' disorder, but, while the majority of clients coming to the attention of care professionals will be female this is certainly not a condition exclusive to women. Borderline personality disorder has undergone something of a rebranding process in recent years, and is now increasingly known as emotionally unstable personality disorder. Many believe this is a much more comprehensible, meaningful label.

On the other hand, anti-social personality disorder (ASPD) tends to be more prevalent among men than women, and is particularly common among both remand and sentenced male prisoners. People with ASPD have a typically anti-authoritarian attitude, do not conform to social norms or laws, and have a tendency toward repeated aggressive and upsetting behaviour, with little or no remorse shown or consideration for how their behaviour has affected those around them. They have a flagrant disregard for feelings, and often lie or manipulate situations for personal gain, even when it is obvious that their actions will harm or upset other people. Like other personality disorders, ASPD is an adult condition although diagnosis will also depend on disruptive and aggressive behaviour in childhood and adolescence, with school exclusion a very common feature of the person's history.

Cluster C: The 'anxious' and 'fearful' types

Cluster C includes obsessive-compulsive, dependent and avoidant personality disorders. These are possibly the least likely of the personality disorders to be seen in mental health or community services, and will often apply to people living otherwise normal lives, albeit with particular problems in terms of work, relationships and lifestyle.

In many ways, obsessive-compulsive personality disorder is almost a diametrical opposite of dependent personality disorder. The former type might often be seen in those commonly described as 'control freaks', 'workaholics' and 'perfectionists'. In common with other types, obsessive-compulsive personality disorder is characterised by an inability to show tenderness or warmth to others or to trust anyone else but themselves with even the simplest of tasks. Individuals become obsessed with work or in some cases, hobbies and interests, often to the exclusion of all else. They are unhappy with anything less than complete perfection in a given task or piece of work, which must be 'just right' with nothing left to chance.

On the other hand, people with dependent personality disorder are excessively passive, handing responsibility for every area of life to other people. They have little self-confidence and are often completely unable to function independently, often depending almost entirely on the care of a relative or partner for even the simplest of responsibilities. It is not uncommon for someone with this disorder to have no conception of, for example, a bank account or how to pay household bills, they will often remain non-drivers throughout their lives and may remain deliberately unemployed while living on the means of those that are supporting them.

Treating personality disorder

Personality-disordered individuals present enormous difficulties and challenges to mental health workers, and invariably spark debate as to the validity of categorising personality in terms of 'normal' or 'abnormal'. Furthermore, mental health professionals often disagree on the 'treatability' of personality disorder, although it is widely acknowledged that in-patient units seldom provide anything other than short-term respite or crisis intervention for patients. These arguments have contributed to something of a 'postcode lottery' in terms of the treatment and resources available to this client group. In fact, the extent to which personality-disordered people can access appropriate services depends largely on the extent to which local resources both acknowledge personality disorder, and believe that such individuals can be successfully helped (National Institute for Mental Health in England 2003).

This state of affairs has prompted recent high-level initiatives to encourage local providers to develop specialised services for this client group, with increased funding for resources and care packages based on an increasingly solid evidence base for effective treatment and support.

While it is certainly the case that the resources outlined here are specialised, scarce and demanding of intensive extra training, approaches such as these are coming under increasing scrutiny and research, and in the absence of an effective and specific drug treatment for personality disorder, the 'talking treatments' along with the often invaluable contribution of the housing and community care agencies represent an increasingly optimistic outlook on what used to be described as the 'diagnosis of exclusion'.

We shall outline some of the more well-established approaches, and while they differ in theoretical basis and method, some common underlying principles have been described that appear to be constant in the more promising approaches.

They tend to be well-structured, have a clear focus, emphasise the importance of compliance with the therapy, and must actually 'make sense' to the patient. Furthermore, the treatments that garner the most optimism tend to emphasise the attachment between therapist and patient, are relatively long-term in nature, and are well integrated with other services with which the recipient might be involved.

The therapeutic community approach

Therapeutic communities are perhaps the oldest and most well established of treatments for personality disorder, although it could be argued that they represent an 'approach' rather than a psychiatric treatment in the usual sense. The story of their development is surprising. Faced with the prospect of treating huge numbers of combat-traumatised soldiers during the Second World War, military psychiatrists Tom Main and Maxwell Jones established communities at military hospitals in Birmingham and North London respectively, where the boundaries of traditional doctor–nurse–patient roles became increasingly unimportant against a backdrop of shared experiences and group discussion.

Both Main and Jones continued their work long after the war had ended, and founded the Cassel and Henderson Hospitals respectively, both of which continue to this day as important centres of excellence in the treatment of personality disorder. Therapeutic communities are, in essence, small, cohesive communities whose members are made up of both staff and patients, and where all members participate in decision-making, rule formation and the day-to-day running of the community. Group therapy and discussion underpin the day-to-day activities against an ethos of communalism and respect for the behaviour and feelings of others, although anti-social or disruptive actions are discussed and, if necessary, censured by the community. Although the community consists of both 'patients' and paid professional staff, the more traditional inter-discipline hierarchy and boundaries between staff and patients are 'flattened'.

While this approach has helped many thousands of personality-disordered individuals, and studies have suggested optimism in treating those who (in many cases) have been deemed 'untreatable' (Bateman and Tyres 2004), there remain barriers to their wider establishment and development.

First, those most likely to benefit from this approach are in many ways least likely to commit to such a long-term and intensive process, even when they have been referred to a service and accepted by the community itself. Second, therapeutic communities demand a high level of commitment on the part of professional staff, who must be prepared to work in ways that vary widely from the more traditional models of psychiatric care to which they may be accustomed.

Nonetheless, the therapeutic community approach has now been applied to an increasingly wide variety of settings, such as daycare centres and even the prison system, and while the success of treatment has yet to be unequivocally proven by rigorous research (Rutter and Tyrer 2003) there remains both optimism and anecdotal evidence for the efficacy of this approach.

The cognitive approach

The cognitive approach to therapy with personality-disordered people encompasses several different types of talking treatment that are currently being researched and validated in terms of their usefulness for this client group. The best known of these is cognitive behaviour therapy (CBT: see Chapter 2) but other variations on the cognitive theme, where patients are helped to examine and modify their own thoughts and feelings by a trained therapist, have emerged in recent years as potentially useful means of addressing personality disorder.

DIALECTICAL BEHAVIOUR THERAPY (DBT)

Although DBT was initially developed to treat women with borderline personality disorder, with a specific remit to reduce incidents of self-harm and stabilise chaotic lifestyles, recent initiatives are now underway to widen its remit to male patients and to address other forms of personality disorder.

DBT is usually a group-oriented therapy, and in many ways is reminiscent of a training course. One of the key aspects of personality disorder is the fact that many of those identified as having this condition are never aware, or never accept that they have been diagnosed or labelled in this way. One of the aims of DBT is to educate group members about their disorder, as well as looking at their own feelings and behaviours in detail and learning new coping skills to cope with stress, and replace familiar responses such as self-harm, substance abuse or aggression.

Based on a core principle of positive relationships between clients and their specially trained therapists, DBT has yet to be thoroughly and independently researched although initial results and anecdotal evidence have suggested some possibilities, particularly in reduction of critical incidents such as self-harm (Bateman and Tyrer 2004).

COGNITIVE ANALYTICAL THERAPY (CAT)

Recent years have seen a growing interest in the use of this therapy in addressing the problems associated with borderline personality disorder. When applied in this context, CAT is based on the theory that BPD represents a set of 'self-states'. In other words, the person experiences a number of distinct moods and behaviours and rapidly swings between these states according to external influences, such as stress, relationships or tasks. The person has little or no ability to control their emotions as they switch from one 'self-state' to another, and therapy is essentially a working collaboration between therapist and patient in which the latter's self-states are identified in both day-to-day life and within the therapy sessions themselves.

CAT integrates cognitive and psychoanalytic ideas, although the emphasis is firmly on description and the 'here and now' as opposed to the interpretation and reflection more readily associated with psychoanalysis. CAT is structured and time-limited, with pen-and-paper exercises and homework representing much of the therapeutic body of the treatment. There is as yet little empirical evidence for the efficacy of this approach, although a number of studies are in progress to evaluate the use of CAT with personality-disordered individuals in a variety of settings.

Pharmacological treatments

Given the lack of resources and difficulties in applying some or all of the types of talking treatments outlined above, and the occasional necessity of admitting personality-disordered patients to psychiatric units in times of crisis, it is unsurprising that drug treatments (such as anti-depressants, anti-psychotics and mood stabilisers) are a frequently used resource despite the lack of a specific treatment for this condition and the general reluctance to further 'medicalise' personality disorder or induce dependence on the part of patients. However, personality disorder is often associated with 'comorbid' conditions such as depression or anxiety, which can be treated successfully with medication, and limited and careful prescription of SSRI anti-depressants and anxiolytics has been seen to have some part to play in the treatment of specific problem behaviours and the resolution of short-term distress or crisis, which may require considerable 'damping' before the individual can begin to work in a more psychological way or respond to professionals using the interpersonal skills outlined elsewhere in this chapter.

Working with personality disorder

Personality-disordered individuals present enormous difficulties and challenges to mental health workers, and invariably spark debate as to the validity of categorising personality in terms of 'normal' or 'abnormal'. Furthermore, mental health professionals often disagree on the 'treatability' of personality disorder, although it is widely acknowledged that in-patient units seldom provide anything other than short-term respite or crisis intervention for patients.

In fact, the extent to which personality-disordered people can access appropriate services depends largely on the extent to which local resources both acknowledge personality disorder, and believe that such individuals can be successfully helped (National Institute for Mental Health in England 2003). This state of affairs has prompted high-level initiatives to encourage local providers to develop specialised services for this client group, with increased funding for resources and care packages based on an increasingly solid evidence base for effective treatment and support (NICE 2009a; 2009b).

Specific skills-based and group approaches such as dialectical behaviour therapy (DBT) and the therapeutic community have generated the most hopeful evidence of effecting positive change in personality disorder. But for most service users, access to such services varies widely, may be subject to long waiting lists, or may not be suitable. For social care workers, it is more useful to focus on the interpersonal skills and factors that have been found to have a positive effect with service users, and that can be part of our day-to-day work with personality-disordered people.

The list that follows is a compilation of anecdotal observations and the research findings of dozens of studies from the last 25 years (Bateman and Tyrer, 2004; Gask, Evans and Kessler 2013; Warren *et al.* 2003).

- *There is cause for hope and optimism.* Working with people who have lived with a very different set of values, beliefs and behaviours to our own can be exceptionally challenging. This is particularly so when staff are faced with the full range of difficulties and obstacles the service user can present. In fact, not every worker can deal with personality-disordered people.

  While there are no well-evidenced 'gold standard' treatments for personality disorder, there is certainly evidence (both empirical and anecdotal) that staff and services approaching service users with some if not all of the attributes listed here can make significant improvements. With personality disorder we measure improvements in terms of time spent out of prison or in-patient admission, or a reduction in the frequency and severity of the sort of life crisis that may have otherwise punctuated the service user's life with monotonous regularity.

  When learners report in training that the only apparent achievement thus far is that a service user is 'still alive', we can often qualify this statement by suggesting that a service or individual has reduced the potential for that individual's very high-risk behaviour to have killed them. This, in the world of personality disorder, is a significant achievement.

- *We need to think in the long term.* We'll remember from the definitions earlier that personality disorder is an enduring, inflexible way of dealing with the world that has developed over a lifetime. Studies consistently suggest the very long periods of time required for service users to gain trust and stability in order for any meaningful support to take place.

- *An emphasis on compliance/adherence is useful.* Psychological treatments for borderline personality disorder such as dialectical behaviour therapy (DBT) place great emphasis on attendance at groups and appointments with staff. This places boundaries around the professional relationship. The service user can choose to stay within the boundaries and receive the support on offer. Alternatively they may decide not to adhere to what has been agreed, in which case we may decide that this service at this time isn't going to be appropriate for this particular service user.

- *It is difficult to build trusting relationships.* Service users often come from chaotic, transient backgrounds and may have difficulties trusting new people. New keyworkers may represent the latest in a long line of failed professional relationships and may be 'tested' by the service user to assess the worker's ability to tolerate the attitudes, behaviours and beliefs that may well have sabotaged previous attempts at help and support from other services.

- *It is important to be accessible, consistent and reliable.* Many teams with experience of working with personality-disordered people will have experience of 'splitting' and 'manipulation' by such individuals. These are tools developed since early childhood, and a service user can be extremely skilful in causing dissent within teams and creating difficulties for individual workers.

Consistency of approach, and consistency between team members and services reduces the potential for sabotage. Services and individual should be accessible and available when they say they will be available, without being at the 'beck and call' of the service user. The setting of clear boundaries is key to successful engagement and rapport-forming with service users who are often suspicious, chaotic and unboundaried.

- *Being well integrated with other agencies will reduce problems.* There are a number of factors that determine whether a service user is or isn't known to mental health services. However, attachments to multiple services is a frequent scenario and, in some cases, this can lead to miscommunication. Situations involving one worker being 'played off' against another are not uncommon.

  The evidence suggests that support plans involving more than one individual or agency (e.g. a GP, social worker or mental health advocate) work best when all parties plus the service user are very clear about what is expected of whom, and who is responsible for what.

- *Well-structured plans with clear goals have the best chance of success.* We'll have seen from what we've covered and discussed so far that personality-disordered service users have often led chaotic lives focused on very short-term goals and devoid of purpose or structure. Supportive professional relationships have been shown to have the most success with an emphasis on clearly planned, unambiguous and focused interventions where both service user and worker(s) are very clear about what we hope to achieve together, and how that relationship is going to progress.

Plans may include goals as simple as paying rent on time every month, or attending a college course every Tuesday, but need to be achievable, realistic and demonstrable, leaving little room for debate or obfuscation.

- *Careful management of 'endings' and transitions to other agencies or practitioners will avoid difficulties.* We have already seen how personality disorder work is by default a long-term commitment, and important consistency can be in maintaining a successful support relationship. Another factor identified by Bateman and Tyrer (2004) is that of 'constancy' – having a professional relationship with a worker who is going to be around for a period of time and can successfully manage the various pitfalls and challenges presented by that individual.

  Key staff and keyworkers will of course move on from time to time, and this needs to be managed extremely carefully. This is a group of people who perhaps won't understand a worker's career choices or their decision to retire. They are accustomed to abandonment and may see the termination of a professional relationship as yet another example of being cast adrift.

  Anecdotal experience suggests a gradual transition of support to other workers or agencies, with care taken not to make changes to support plans or contingencies until a well-planned handover has taken place.

The Personality Disorder Toolkit

Personality-disordered clients of health, social and non-statutory services are almost universally unpopular with workers. Faced with an array of complex needs, challenging situations and sometimes threatening and dangerous behaviours, it is little wonder that staff are often left feeling helpless, de-skilled and, in some cases, 'burnt out'. The Personality Disorder Toolkit is simply an array of roles, tips and techniques that can be used in day-to-day practice with difficult situations and individuals. None of these tools are instant panaceas or 'magic wands', but used consistently over a period of time within a stable environment professional relationship and with adequate support and supervision from colleagues, the Toolkit is certainly a means of addressing some of the more problematic behaviours encountered in work with this client group.

The Fencemaker

Personality-disordered clients will often have a different view of the social norms that others might take for granted. The setting of clear boundaries is important for both worker and client so that both parties know 'where they stand'. Rules and boundaries are important, but it is essential that there are good reasons for their existence, which should be explained clearly and unambiguously. It is also important that there is consistency within the staff group. If boundaries are interpreted differently between one staff member and another this can lead to confusion and ambiguity, a situation that may well be exploited by the client, leading to further confusion and confrontation.

The Director

One of the key features of personality disorder is the individual's inclination toward impulsivity, having a tendency to react to situations without pausing for thought or consideration of consequences. The Director seeks to help the person find alternative strategies to problems (whether real or perceived) and points out how past or present reactions might have led to further problems, whereas a little contemplation and insight might have led to a much improved outcome. Where personality-disordered people often 'act out' their frustration in anti-social or aggressive ways, the Director might also be able to help clients 'playback' their responses to difficult situations, and realise how their behaviour has affected both themselves and others.

The Detective

Another key feature of his disorder is 'black and white thinking', or in other words taking the view of situations or people being either 'very good' or 'very bad' with little or no 'medium'. The Detective encourages the client to 'test the evidence' before coming to extreme conclusions, and suggests they try to see the 'bigger picture' of a scenario.

The Telescope

The Telescope is all about making small, distant objects appear much closer. Personality-disordered people often have little ability to identify their feelings or process emotions in the same way as most people. When asked how they feel, a typical response might be 'don't know' or they might query the relevance of the question. The Telescope monitors non-verbal cues and points these out, albeit with tact and a non-judgemental approach. A response such as 'You're looking a little miserable today' might lead to further exploration of why the person appears the way they do, particularly where the worker has an established rapport with the client and knows enough about their circumstances and behaviour to be able to draw out more expression and insight from that person than might otherwise be possible.

The Straight Bat

The Straight Bat represents a straightforward personal style as a response to clients who might be distrustful and manipulative in an attempt to maintain some semblance of order and control in an otherwise chaotic life. The Straight Bat presents a positive role model and takes a calm but robust stance to anti-social or threatening behaviours. Whereas it is sometimes tempting and all too easy for workers to become drawn into crises or problematic situations, the Straight Bat remains objective and tries to help the person resolve their own problems while remaining 'offstage' themselves.

A further part of the role involves honesty. It is surprisingly (but understandably) common for staff to tell 'white lies' or withhold information in order to avert a crisis or to prevent the client 'acting out', perhaps in response to bad news. The short-term gains of such action are seldom rewarded by longer-term progress, and it frequently leads to further conflict and an opportunity for personality-disordered clients to cause conflict within a staff group.

The Forcefield

Working in mental health is as different from working in a shop or an office as playing football in a back garden is from appearing in an FA Cup Final. Staff invest a considerable part of themselves, their own lives and their own personalities into the work they do, and nowhere is this more true than working with personality disorder. The development of a rapport with a damaged, distrustful person who has spent many years unable to form meaningful relationships with others can be ultimately rewarding. However, it is not uncommon for workers to allow personal and professional boundaries to become blurred, often with the effect of a parent/child scenario developing. The Forcefield is about clarifying these personal/professional boundaries from the outset, and defining relationship expectations at an early stage. If clients are to be helped develop their own coping and problem-solving skills for the future, staff members need to avoid the temptation to become over-involved while encouraging the individual to address their own problems, albeit with sound advice and encouragement. The Forcefield is also aware of the crucial importance of supervision from peers and managers, whether on a formal or 'ad hoc' basis.

The Ray of Light

The Ray of Light is aware that even the most difficult clients are also capable of being genuinely likeable, humorous and, in some cases, talented people. These attributes can be highlighted and encouraged. However, for many individuals with personality disorder, a life of chaos and unhappiness is familiar and comforting. Making progress and moving forward may often be interspersed with periods of unease and uncertainty. The Ray of Light is aware of this, and even anticipates and is prepared for occasional retreats into the 'comfort zone' by way of a return to familiar behaviours and attitudes. Many workers respond with disappointment when this happens. 'Just when we thought we were getting somewhere' is a familiar phrase in this scenario, but the Ray of Light remains optimistic, does not panic and continues using the array of tools outlined here. Pragmatism sometimes dictates that the client is not yet ready for permanent change, but often 'relapse' is short-lived and can be seen as a valuable learning experience.

CASENOTES: WORKING WITH PERSONALITY DISORDER

Peter

Peter is the middle child of three siblings. When his younger sister was born his mother developed post-natal depression and found it impossible to cope with three small children. Peter was over-active as a child and wanted constant attention. If this was not immediately given, he had temper tantrums and was aggressive and destructive, prompting his mother to give in to his demands rather than risk a confrontation.

Peter's father was often away on business, but when he was at home his parents constantly argued and he often witnessed his father hitting his mother. At school, Peter was regularly in trouble for fighting, and was excluded at the age of seven for assaulting a teacher. Peter's parents were increasingly unable to cope with his behaviour by this time, and he was placed with foster parents and referred to a child psychologist. With the help of the psychologist, his foster parents established firm boundaries from the onset to which Peter responded well.

After a year Peter returned to live with his mother. His parents had separated whilst he had been in foster care, and he did not see his father again until he was 16. Within weeks of returning home, Peter's violent arguments with his mother began again. At the age of ten Peter began mixing with a group of 12-year-olds, staying out until late at night and smoking cigarettes and drinking alcohol, which led to his first police caution for shoplifting at the age of 11.

He reacted violently whenever his mother tried to prevent him leaving the house, and ignored her pleas for him to return home at a reasonable time. Peter's mother never reported the assaults to the police. At the age of 11 Peter began using Ecstasy and amphetamines. Initially he funded this by shoplifting and stealing money from his mother's purse. In time he began to sell drugs to local schoolchildren. By this time Peter was a pupil at a special needs school, but was an infrequent attender.

At the age of 16 Peter was arrested and charged with aggravated burglary. Whilst on bail he took a paracetamol overdose, and was seen by a psychiatrist who prescribed anti-depressants and offered him out-patient appointments, which he did not to attend.

Peter received his first custodial sentence at the age of 17. Since then he has been a sentenced prisoner several times and spent long periods as a remand prisoner, mainly because he fails to comply with the conditions of bail or community sentence orders. When in prison Peter spends a lot of time in segregation for assaults on other prisoners and officers.

Peter's relationships have mainly been of short duration. The longest lasted six months and ended when he was sent to prison for assaulting her whilst she was pregnant with his child. Peter has never seen his child who is now five years old. Peter has not seen his parents or sisters for a number of years, and he has few friends other than several criminal associates.

In addition to spending periods in custody Peter has also had a number of admissions to psychiatric units as a result of taking overdoses. These admissions are often of short duration because of Peter's disruptive behaviour, often fuelled by drugs or alcohol. He rarely attends out-patient appointments.

Peter's most recent conviction was for a serious assault on a nurse whilst under the influence of alcohol, for which he received a two-year custodial sentence. Whilst serving this sentence he became severely depressed and was assessed by the prison's mental health in-reach team and admitted to a secure psychiatric unit.

At the onset of this admission Peter attempted to intimidate and manipulate the nursing staff as he had done on previous admissions. However, unlike his previous admissions, the multi-disciplinary team set firm boundaries on his behaviour.

Initially Peter was only allowed to leave the ward with a nurse escort. Visitors to the ward were vetted by the multi-disciplinary team so he had no access to drugs and alcohol. He soon discovered that the staff checked everything he said with each other. Any changes to his treatment were discussed and agreed by the team. He was also encouraged to attend occupational therapy.

Initially Peter reacted against the treatment programme. However, he soon found that he achieved more by co-operating with the team rather than trying to fight against them as he had previously done.

Peter's mood began to lift. The multi-disciplinary team decided that Peter could have half-an-hour unescorted leave in the grounds twice a day on the condition that he agreed to random drugs screening. For the first three weeks this went well. Peter returned within the allotted time and the drug screens proved negative.

During the fourth week Peter returned to the ward within the half an hour but in an excited and argumentative mood. A saliva test showed positive for amphetamines and his leave was stopped immediately. On being told this, Peter threw a chair across the room. The police were called and he was charged with criminal damage.

When the effects of the amphetamines had worn off, Peter told the multi-disciplinary team that whilst out in the grounds he decided that 'a line of whizz' would lift his mood so called a friend.

Following several more occasions such as this, Peter claimed that 'something had changed'. He was now 28 and had spent most of his adult life in either hospital or prison. He had re-established contact with his mother and sisters, and had even been able to talk to them about the effect his behaviour had had on them in previous years. After a further six months in hospital the multi-disciplinary team began discussing discharge with Peter, with referral to a therapeutic community being the preferred option for both him and the staff.

Peter was accepted at a therapeutic community but found it difficult fitting in with the group, especially once he discovered that he was the only member of the community that had not been sexually abused. He found it difficult sitting in groups listening to other group members talking of their experiences, and believed he had nothing in common with the other residents. After three weeks he walked out.

Peter returned to his home town and soon returned to his old ways. Within a month he was arrested for burglary and possession with intent to supply. He received a custodial sentence, became severely depressed and was referred to the psychiatrist under whose care he had been during his last hospital admission. This time he was treated in prison by the prison's mental health in-reach team. Prior to his release a Care Programme Approach meeting was held and a care co-ordinator was allocated to him. On release from prison Peter went to live in a supported hostel for ex-offenders.

The hostel imposed firm boundaries and Peter was asked to sign an abstinence agreement as a condition of tenancy. He agreed to his care co-ordinator carrying out regular drug screens and attended regular appointments with the psychiatrist.

Peter has been at the hostel for 18 months now. He has a small circle of friends, and works as a labourer for a local builder, which at the age of 31 is his first ever paid employment. He is also attending an evening computer course at college. He is in regular contact with his family and has recently met his daughter for the first time. The next challenge for Peter will be moving into independent accommodation.

Peter: Points for reflection

1. Which factors in Peter's early life might have caused difficulties for him in adulthood?

2. Like many people with a personality disorder, Peter is not formally 'diagnosed' as such. Is there sufficient evidence for a personality disorder to be identified, and if so, what difference might this make to his support and treatment?

3. What are Peter's needs?

4. Which aspects of Peter's care (both in hospital and in the supported housing) have most benefited him in the long term?

References

American Psychiatric Association (2013) *Diagnostic and Statistical Manual of Mental Disorders* (5th edn). Arlington, VA: American Psychiatric Publishing.

Babiak, P. and Hare, R. (2007) *Snakes in Suits: When Psychopaths Go to Work.* New York: HarperBusiness.

Bateman, A.W. and Tyrer, P. (2004) 'Psychological treatment for borderline personality disorders.' *Advances in Psychiatric Treatment 10*, 378–388.

Bolton, W., Lovell, K., Morgan, L. and Wood, H. (2014) *Meeting the Challenge, Making a Difference: Working Effectively to Support People with Personality Disorder in the Community.* Available at www.emergenceplus.org.uk/images/Documents/meeting-the-challenge-making-a-difference-practitioner-guide.pdf.

Bowden-Jones, O., Iqbal, M.Z., Tyrer, P. *et al.* (2004) 'Prevalence of personality disorder in alcohol and drug services and associated comorbidity.' *Addiction 99*, 10, 1306–1314.

Craissati, J., Minoudis, P., Shaw, J., Chuan, S.J. *et al.* (2013) *Working with Personality Disordered Offenders. A Practitioner's Guide.* London: Ministry of Justice. Available at www.dh.gov.uk/prod_consum_dh/groups/dh_digitalassets/documents/digitalasset/dh_124319.pdf.

Gask, L., Evans, M. and Kessler, D. (2013) 'Clinical review: Personality disorder.' *BMJ 347*, f5276.

Huang, Y., Kotov, R., de Girolamo, G., Preti, A. *et al.* (2009) 'DSM-IV personality disorders in the WHO World Mental Health Surveys.' *British Journal of Psychiatry 195*, 46–53.

National Collaborating Centre for Mental Health (2013) *Antisocial Personality Disorder: The NICE Guideline on Treatment, Management and Prevention.* National Clinical Practice Guideline Number 77. The British Psychological Society and The Royal College of Psychiatrists.

National Institute for Mental Health in England (2003) *Personality Disorder: No Longer a Diagnosis of Exclusion.* London: Department of Health.

NICE (2009a) *Antisocial Personality Disorder: Treatment, Management and Prevention.* NICE Clinical Guideline 77. London: National Institute for Health and Care Excellence. Available at www.nice.org.uk/guidance/cg77.

NICE (2009b) *Borderline Personality Disorder: Treatment and Management.* NICE Clinical Guideline 78. London: National Institute for Health and Care Excellence. Available at www.nice.org.uk/guidance/cg78.

Ronson, J. (2012) *The Psychopath Test.* London: Picador.

Rutter, D. and Tyrer, P. (2003) 'The value of therapeutic communities in the treatment of personality disorder: A suitable place for treatment?' *Journal of Psychiatric Practice 9*, 291–302.

Viding, E. (2013) 'Callous unemotional traits in children.' *Observer.* Association of Psychological Science. Available at www.psychologicalscience.org/index. php/publications/observer/2013/october-13/callous-unemotional-traits-in-children.html.

Warren, F., Preedy-Fayers, K., McGauley, G., Pickering, A. *et al.* (2003) *Review of Treatments for Severe Personality Disorder.* London: Home Office.

Weaver, T., Madden, P., Charles, V. *et al.* (2003) 'Comorbidity of substance misuse and mental illness in community mental health and substance misuse services.' *British Journal of Psychiatry 183*, 304–313.

World Health Organization (1992) *ICD-10: Classification of Mental and Behavioural Disorders.* Geneva: WHO.

Chapter 6

MENTAL ILLNESS AND THE CRIMINAL JUSTICE SYSTEM

My son did not cope well in prison. Care for the mentally ill should be therapeutic and in surroundings conducive to peace and recovery – not the barred, noisy, stressful and gardenless prison. Those of you who have visited prisons will be aware of how unpleasant and entirely unsuitable a place they are for the mentally ill. My son was not a criminal; he was in prison because there was no alternative place of safety. (Prison Reform Trust/National Federation of Women's Institutes 2014)

The above is a quote from a WI member whose son committed suicide in prison. It was one of many such deaths, but led to the creation of a campaigning coalition called Care Not Custody. But for many mentally ill people, particularly those living chaotic, marginalised lives, custody is perhaps the only means available of receiving any care at all. For those who struggle or are reluctant to access help from a GP, the police and paramedics have become their de facto primary care service. With mental health beds, staff and resources reduced to the barest minimum, the criminal justice system has become in many ways the 'new asylum'.

People with mental health issues can come to the criminal justice system in one of two ways. Section 136 of the Mental Health Act allows police officers to convey a person they suspect of having a mental illness to a 'place of safety'. This ought to be a hospital environment – a psychiatric unit preferably, or the emergency department of a local hospital where patients can receive a psychiatric assessment. Officers can use the police station cells as a last resort, but evidence suggests this is all too often the first line of action, with vulnerable people sometimes spending many hours in custody despite not having committed any offence (HMIC 2013). Regular readers of the excellent Mental Health Cop blog (http://mentalhealthcop.wordpress.com) will be familiar with some of the problems faced by police officers and custody sergeants in these situations. Police officers and paramedics receive precious little training in mental health awareness despite taking an increasingly 'front-line' role in bringing distressed, vulnerable people into an environment where they may eventually receive some degree of care. With the majority of section 136 detentions and street incidents happening at night, statutory health and social services can be difficult to access, leaving people in custody for many hours before being assessed and hopefully relocated to a more appropriate environment.

The other way that people with mental health issues come to the criminal justice system is after arrest. For those arrested as a result of what are usually minor offences, the police have access to Forensic Medical Examiners who can perform what is usually a rudimentary assessment by a non-psychiatrically trained doctor. Under the Police and Criminal Evidence Act (PACE) the custody sergeant is obliged to find an advocate to represent the detainee during interview, referred to as the 'appropriate adult' (AA). Provision of the AA is sometimes arranged by charities or local advocacy services, but there remain no statutory guidelines for this service and provision is patchy (Prison Reform Trust/ National Federation of Women's Institutes 2014).

There are however several successful new schemes to provide criminal justice liaison and diversion services at as early a stage as possible. Street triage nurses accompany police officers to situations that may involve vulnerable or mentally ill people, or can assess defendants at the police station, providing both a level of expertise and experience not usually available to police officers. This sort of scheme also means that (in theory at least) histories can be traced and other professionals contacted who may be able to provide more appropriate services for that individual than further involvement with the criminal justice system (Durcan *et al.* 2014).

For those who are charged with an offence, a magistrates court has several options for defendants identified as having mental health problems. There is the promising yet seldom used Mental Health Treatment Requirement, which allows for a minor offence to be dealt with by way of a community sentence and an agreement to receive intervention from local mental health services. Take-up of this little-known provision has, for a number of reasons, been poor to say the least (Scott and Moffatt 2012). In some cases a magistrates court can arrange for mental health assessment prior to sentencing, and can send a defendant to hospital as an alternative to a prison sentence. This is an ideal solution that for many represents 'first contact' with mental health services and a beginning of resolution of mental health problems that may have been problematic for many years.

Unfortunately, in-patient beds are seldom available or are available at private units many miles away from any family or social attachment that individual had with a community. All too often magistrates resort to a prison sentence, or a community order under the supervision of a probation officer who will seldom have the appropriate training to deal with the complexities of mentally ill offenders despite a mental illness incidence of 39 per cent among the caseloads of most probation services (Brooker *et al.* 2012).

For those given a custodial sentence at a jail that may be many miles from the prisoner's locality, screening will take place as the person first comes into the prison. This is often a busy, somewhat chaotic environment where an initial mental health assessment is often carried out by a health care worker with little psychiatric experience.

The often harsh environment of prison serves to exacerbate existing issues; but for some, mental health problems emerge for the first time behind the stone walls and steel doors. The statistics are dramatic but no longer surprising. The majority of prisoners have some form of mental health problem, but 70 per cent have at least two co-occurring disorders, frequently involving substance misuse (Singleton, Meltzer and Gatward 1998). A staggering 30 per cent of female prisoners (and 10 per cent of men) have had in-patient psychiatric treatment prior to imprisonment (Department of Health 2007). Two thirds of all prisoners meet diagnostic criteria for personality disorder (Singleton *et al.* 1998).

The National Health Service took responsibility for all prison health care in 2006. Mental health inreach teams work with prison health care staff and prison officers to provide assessment and liaison with other professionals and agencies. Opportunities for treatment are limited by a number of factors, not the least of which is the frequent movement of prisoners between prisons and the difficulty in doing any long-term psychological work within the constraints of time and resources. Mentally ill prisoners can be treated with medication should they wish, but severely unwell individuals cannot be sectioned in prison and cannot be given medication against their will. It is perhaps unsurprising that many vulnerable prisoners spend much of their sentence in 'seg' or a segregation unit, away from the noise and turbulence of the general wings and the potential for conflict with other prisoners reacting to what might be bizarre, incomprehensible behaviour.

Inreach professionals spend much of their time attempting to arrange aftercare for prisoners who are often spending quite short periods of time incarcerated. The Care Programme Approach provides a structure for all patients receiving care from mental health professionals to receive some form of care plan, and long-term support, in particular for those with severe and enduring mental illness. Making such arrangements for prisoners is often less than easy. Community Mental Health Teams can prove remarkably reluctant to take responsibility for prisoners after release (Durcan and Knowles 2006; Sainsbury Centre 2000).

The immediate aftermath of release can be a particularly stressful time for those who have very little to be released into. Suicide rates are worryingly high in the days and weeks following release (Pratt *et al.* 2006), with many prisoners wishing to stay locked up in a place they feel offers comparative stability and safety. For many vulnerable prisoners, life in the community means little by way of help for mental health problems, poor or non-existent housing, and exposure to most of the same pitfalls and stresses (such as drugs or alcohol) from which prison has provided at least some protection. For this is a criminal justice system that, despite a slew of reports and recommendations in recent years, is still often unwilling or unable to provide joined-up, patient-focused services for the mentally ill. For many, it is custody not care that has become the new asylum.

A whistle-stop tour of the criminal justice system ———

Here we offer basic explanations of some of the most important terminology that readers may come across when working with offenders with mental heath issues.

We will use the term mentally disordered offender (MDO) rather than service user as people with mental health problems who enter the criminal justice system do not choose to use the services with whom they come into contact. In a large number of cases the type of offending behaviour that brings an MDO to the attention of the criminal justice system are the more minor offences. As one psychiatrist put it many years ago, 'the MDO is more likely to be stealing the milk for their cereal than to be a serial killer'.

Background

In 2005 the Department of Health and National Institute for Mental Health published *The Offender Mental Health Care Pathway* (DoH/NIMH 2005). This important document provided a structure and process to the development of services for MDOs at all points and throughout their journey in the criminal justice system. It identified who was responsible for each part of the process and involved clinicians, health service managers and commissioners.

Until the publication of *The Offender Mental Health Care Pathway* the provision of services had always been somewhat ad hoc, with great geographical disparity about what was available for offenders in different parts of the country. Since 2005 the implementation of *The Offender Mental Health Care Pathway* has been further supported by the recommendations outlined in the 2009 Bradley Report (Department of Health 2009).

Arrest and the police station
POLICE AND CRIMINAL EVIDENCE ACT
For all mentally disordered offenders entry into the criminal justice system will begin with their arrest and being taken to a police station. All offenders held in police custody are subject to

the Police and Criminal Evidence Act 1984, otherwise known as PACE. This legislation has its own code of practice and provides protection for the police, offender and public. It covers everything from obtaining evidence to arrest, interviewing and how long a suspect can be held before being charged.

If no charge has been made within the set timeframe, the suspect has to be released, although in exceptional circumstances the police can apply to a court for extra time to question the suspect. Failure to comply with PACE can result in the discontinuation of a prosecution.

APPROPRIATE ADULT

Under Code C of PACE children, juveniles and anyone thought to have a learning disability or mental disorder has to have an 'appropriate adult' present when being questioned. In the case of people with suspected mental health problems or adults with a learning disability, the appropriate adult can be a parent or friend, but will most often come from an advocacy service, social services or a Community Mental Health Team. They are required to be present during police procedures, such as obtaining samples for evidence and questioning, and are there to ensure that the suspect is not put under unnecessary stress, and that they understand what is happening to them and why they are there.

CUSTODY SERGEANT

When a suspect is brought into custody it is the custody sergeant who is responsible for the well-being of the suspect while they are in the custody suite. The custody sergeant is also responsible for ensuring that correct legal process is followed and that the PACE code of conduct is adhered to, including the statutory record keeping and time constraints. The custody sergeant has to be satisfied that a suspect is well enough to be in custody. If there are concerns, then he or she will arrange either a medical or mental health assessment.

FORENSIC MEDICAL EXAMINER (FME)

The FME was previously known as the police surgeon and is a doctor independent of the police. The FME will have undertaken specific additional training for the role, including the taking of samples of bodily fluids for analysis. They will also be approved under section 12 of the Mental Health Act 1983, which means they can assess and detain people with a mental illness as defined in the Mental Health Act. The FME not only assesses the physical and mental health needs of suspects, but also provides any immediate treatment. They will advise the custody sergeant of the suspect's fitness to be in custody when required and may obtain samples such as blood and urine for forensic analysis and evidence.

CUSTODY LIAISON TEAMS

Custody liaison teams are teams consisting of mental health nurses, social workers and in some cases psychiatrists that work in police stations and provide mental health screening and assessments to suspects. Their role is to identify suspects who are experiencing acute symptoms of mental illness and arrange transfer to a hospital bed where indicated. This should not affect any prosecution. They also signpost suspects to community services, and if they are already under the care of a Community Mental Health Team, inform the team of the suspect's arrest and assist with liaising and information sharing between the team and the police. They can also alert the court liaison team of the possible need for further assessment and risks.

The first custody liaison teams were developed mainly in inner-city areas in the early 1990s. Their development nationally was a recommendation of the 1992 Reed Report (Department of Health and Home Office 1992) and The National Service Framework, but development was slow. *The Offender Mental Health Care Pathway* and Bradley Report (2009) have made further recommendations that all police custody suites should have access to liaison and diversion services.

Bail, Cautions, Charges, Remand and Sentence

As we have already established, under PACE the police can only hold a suspect for a specified amount of time before having to charge or release the suspect. One option available to the police is to bail a suspect for a specified amount of time while they continue to investigate the case and gather evidence. The suspect then returns to the police station and is either charged or released. To be eligible for bail the police have to be satisfied that the suspect will not commit further offences. Specific conditions can be attached to bail.

Cautions are a type of disposal that the police can consider for minor offences where it may not be in the public interest to prosecute. Cautions are recorded but do not result in a criminal record.

Charge is the term used when the police have evidence that the alleged offence was committed by the suspect. At this stage we use the term 'alleged' because the suspect has not been convicted and could later be found to be innocent. A formal police charge will result in a court appearance.

Bail can be granted whilst further evidence is gathered and an investigation takes place. Everyone has a right to bail, but the decision to grant is based on a risk assessment by police officers. Conditions can be placed on bail. For example, the suspect may be prohibited from contacting another person (such as a victim) or may be barred from visiting certain locations. Any breach of bail could result in a remand in custody as can committing further offences whilst on bail.

To be remanded to prison a suspect has to go before a magistrates court. Suspects are usually remanded in custody where there is a high risk of reoffending or the alleged offence is so serious the court has no option to bail that person back into the community. Time spent on remand is usually taken off the eventual sentence.

A sentence is what the court passes when someone has been found guilty and convicted. There are various sentencing options available to the court:

- A *conditional discharge* means that the case has been discharged with conditions applied for a specified length of time.

- *A deferred sentence* can be used when the court is unsure whether the offender will comply with conditions attached to a community sentence, an example of which might be some form of treatment. They are often passed for a six-month period after which the offender returns to court for the final sentence, which, based on their engagement and progress, can be any of the sentencing options.

- *A community service order* specifies a number of hours of community service that have to be completed. Failure to comply can mean that the offender can be taken back to court for further sentencing.

- A *probation order* for a specific length of time. Conditions can be attached to a probation order, such as where a person lives. During the period of the order the offender will be expected to report to the probation officer at specified times. Failure to comply with the probation order can result in the offender being taken back to court for resentencing.

- A *custodial sentence.*

- A *hospital order* under section 37 of the Mental Health Act, open to both magistrates courts and the crown court, with or without a section 41 restriction order, which can be applied only by the crown court.

Section 136 of the Mental Health Act 1983

A person detained under section 136 has not committed an offence. They are not a 'mentally disordered offender'. This a specific section of the Mental Health Act 1983 that enables the police to take a member of the public who is behaving in a way that leads the police officer to believe that the person may have a mental disorder to a place of safety for assessment. The place of safety ought to be a hospital, but unfortunately a growing lack of resources means such facilities are often unavailable and detainees are kept in police cells until more appropriate provisions can be found. Detention under section 136 can be for up to 72 hours, after which the person can either be discharged, reassessed for section 2 or 3 of the Mental Health Act, or remain in hospital as an informal patient.

Crown Prosecution Service

The Crown Prosecution Service (CPS) was established under the Prosecution of Offences Act 1986. It is the service in England and Wales that is responsible for prosecuting criminal cases. It is made up of lawyers who are independent from the police and examine evidence they have collected to decide if there is enough evidence to bring a prosecution to court. Based on that evidence the CPS will decide what the likely charge should be. The CPS also provides advice and support to victims of crime.

In Scotland the Crown Office and Procurator Fiscal Service is the prosecuting authority and is the equivalent of the CPS in England and Wales.

Magistrates court

All criminal prosecutions begin in the magistrates courts. The case can be heard by a panel of three magistrates who are lay people but will have undergone specific training for the role. One of the panel will be the chairman (or woman) of the bench. In some magistrates courts (usually inner-city courts) a case may be heard by one lone magistrate who is a trained lawyer. This is known as a stipendiary magistrate.

The magistrates have the power to fine an offender up to £5000, remand a suspect to prison or pass sentence including a custodial sentence up of to six months for a single offence. They commit more serious cases to a crown court. Magistrates courts typically deal with speeding offences, shoplifting, minor criminal damage and cases of drunk and disorderly.

From a mental health perspective, magistrates also have powers under section 35 of the Mental Health Act to remand someone to hospital for assessment prior to sentencing. If they find a person guilty of an offence punishable by a prison sentence, they can apply section 37 of the Mental Health Act (a hospital order) with or without 'restrictions', according to the seriousness of the offence and the advice of psychiatric reports. Restriction orders can, however, be applied only by the crown court.

In rare circumstances a magistrates court may be asked by a local authority to grant to police and mental health professionals a warrant to enter a person's home under section 135 of the Mental Health Act in order to admit them to hospital for treatment.

Criminal justice liaison teams in court

Criminal justice liaison teams are not new. Some courts have had access to them since the early 1990s, with two of the oldest being at Victoria Law Courts in Birmingham and Bow Street Magistrates Court in London. In 2014 the government committed funding toward the national development of criminal justice liaison teams in courts. The teams can provide an interface between community mental health services and the courts. They can also advise the court and Crown Prosecution Service on how sentencing options may affect someone with mental health problems, and what support is likely to be available. The involvement of the criminal justice liaison team does not mean that the case should be dropped.

In addition to providing on-the-spot assessments and signposting defendants to relevant mental health services the court criminal justice liaison team can ensure that information about a mentally disordered offender is passed on to the prison mental health team if the mentally disordered offender is remanded or sentenced.

References

Brooker, C., Sirdifield, C., Blizard, R., Denney, D. and Pluck, G. (2012) 'Probation and mental illness.' *Journal of Forensic Psychiatry and Psychology 23*, 4, 522–537.

Department of Health and Home Office (1992) *Review of Health and Social Services for Mentally Disordered Offenders and Others Requiring Similar Services.* Final Summary Report (Reed Report). Cm 2088. London: HMSO.

Department of Health (2007) *Sharing Good Practice in Prison Health.* Conference Report, 4/5 June 2007. Available at www.ohrn.nhs.uk/resource/policy/Yorkconferencereport.pdf.

Department of Health (2009) *The Bradley Report: Lord Bradley's review of people with mental health problems or learning disabilities in the criminal justice system.* London: Department of Health.

Department of Health and National Institute for Mental Health in England (2005) *Offender Mental Health Care Pathway.* London: Department for Health.

Durcan, G. and Knowles, K. (2006) *London's Prison Mental Health Services: A Review.* London: Sainsbury Centre for Mental Health.

Durcan, G., Saunders, A., Gadsby, B. and Hazard, A. (2014) *The Bradley Report Five Years On: An Independent Review of Progress to Date and Priorities for Further Development.* London: Centre for Mental Health. Available at www.centreformentalhealth.org.uk/pdfs/Bradley_report_five_years_on.pdf.

HMIC (2013) *A Criminal Use of Police Cells?* London: Her Majesty's Inspectorate of Constabulary.

Pratt, D., Piper, M., Appleby, L., Webb, R. and Shaw, J. (2006) 'Suicide in recently released prisoners: A population-based cohort study.' *Lancet 368*, 9530, 119–123.

Prison Reform Trust/National Federation of Women's Institutes (2014) *Care not Custody*. London: Prison Reform Trust/National Federation of Women's Institutes. Available at www.prisonreformtrust.org.uk/Portals/0/Documents/care%20not%20custody%20coalitionlo.pdf.

Sainsbury Centre (2008) *Short-changed: Spending on Prison Mental Health Care.* London: Sainsbury Centre for Mental Health.

Scott, G. and Moffatt, S. (2012) *The Mental Health Treatment Requirement: Realising a Better Future.* London: Centre for Mental Health. Available at www.centreformentalhealth.org.uk/publications/mhtr_2012.aspx?ID=666.

Singleton, N., Meltzer, H. and Gatward, R. (1998) *Psychiatric Morbidity among Prisoners in England and Wales.* London: Office for National Statistics.

Chapter 7

INTRODUCING THE MENTAL HEALTH LEGISLATION

Each year in England approximately 25,000 people are subject to the Mental Health Act (HCSIC 2014). It is a common misconception that the MHA exists for the sole purpose of 'locking people up'. However, the MHA is far more complex and wide-ranging than this, encompassing guidance and legislation on many aspects of care, the rights of patients and their families, and the responsibilities of professionals. The MHA provides the legal framework that not only protects the rights of patients, but also professionals and the public. It is also important to remember that the legal powers outlined here apply to clearly designated settings, such as hospitals and statutory services, and in almost all circumstances cannot be enforced in community settings, such as patients' homes, group homes or supported accommodation.

Mental Health Act 1983

The MHA is divided into ten 'parts' and has 149 'sections', each of which is divided into subsections. This chapter will refer only to the most commonly used sections, and those that readers are most likely to see referred to in reports and correspondence.

In 2007 a number of amendments to the 1983 MHA were made, including changes in terminology and its application. The 2007 amendments have not replaced the 1983 Act, but has amended some of its sections, making them more relevant to mental health care in the 21st century. The amendments introduced nine key principles as follows:

- A single definition of mental disorder, which is defined as 'any disorder or disability of mind'. This much broader definition includes brain injury and dementia as well as mental illness. Although learning disability is included, the person has to exhibit 'abnormally aggressive or seriously irresponsible behaviour' to be considered for detention. Patients who have substance misuse problems can only be sectioned if they also have a mental illness diagnosis, such as schizophrenia or bipolar disorder

- The abolition of the 'treatability test' as grounds for a Mental Health Act assessment and introduced new criteria. This means that the specific treatment needed by an individual must be available at the facility to which they are being admitted. The definition of 'treatment' is now broader and does not apply solely to taking medication, a major criticism of the previous version of the MHA.

- Age-appropriate settings where patients under the age of 18 need to be admitted to hospital. This was introduced to stop the practice of bringing young people into completely inappropriate adult services.

- Broadened professional roles. It is now possible for disciplines other than social workers to train for the Approved Mental Health Professional role (AMHP), and for the Responsible Clinician (RC) to replace the old Responsible Medical Officer (RMO) role and to be able to be a discipline other than a doctor.

- Patients' right to apply to a court to change their nearest relative. Under the 1983 Act identifying the nearest relative was a complicated process. It was even more complicated to replace the nearest relative. Patients now have the right to choose who represents this important role.

- Right to advocacy. All patients who are detained under the Mental Health Act have been given the right to have access to an advocacy service.

- Additional safeguards for patients who have been prescribed ECT. If a patient is detained but has capacity (see below), then they can decide if they have ECT or not. If a patient does not have capacity, then they have to be examined by a second opinion doctor. However if a patient has made an advance decision not to have ECT, they cannot be treated against their wishes.

- Community treatment orders. The amendments enable patients who have been detained in hospital to be placed on a community treatment order (CTO). The CTO allows a Responsible Clinician to determine certain conditions by which the patient must abide. Failure to adhere to these conditions may result in a patient being recalled to hospital for treatment, which in practice usually means medication. Patients on a CTO cannot be treated in the community against their will.

- Earlier referral to a Mental Health Review Tribunal.

Terms used in the Mental Health Act

An understanding of the terms used in the Mental Health Act is helpful in working with and supporting those individuals who have been subject to the Act. The MHA has its own terminology referring to very specific legal meanings and powers. Some of these terms may be quite familiar although their exact meaning may be unclear.

SECTION 12 DOCTOR

A 'section 12 doctor' is a doctor who has 'special experience in the diagnosis or treatment of mental disorder'. In practice he or she will normally be a senior psychiatrist and is government approved to make recommendations for the compulsory detention of the mentally ill. Most mental health units have a rota of approved section 12 doctors providing 24-hour availability. Most of the MHA's powers to detain require at least one recommendation from a section 12 doctor.

APPROVED MENTAL HEALTH PROFESSIONAL

'Approved Mental Health Professional' (AMHP) replaced the term Approved Social Worker (ASW). The most noticeable change is that an AMHP no longer needs to be a social worker. The role can be taken by another qualified mental health professional who has undergone specialist training in mental health and mental health law, and has experience of working with the mentally ill or learning disabled. The AMHP co-ordinates the whole process of the Mental Health Act assessment. This includes the identification of two doctors to make an assessment, one of whom must be section 12 qualified. AMHPs look for the least restrictive alternative in assessing and managing a person whose mental illness is causing concern for both their own well-being and that of others. There will be occasions when hospital admission is unavoidable. The AMHP will have to identify a hospital bed and arrange for the patient to be transported to hospital.

The AMHP does not have to be employed by social services but has to be approved by the local authority on whose behalf they carry out the assessment. The expectation on the AMHP is that the assessment is independent. Although the practitioner may be employed by the local NHS Trust, the local authority is responsible for ensuring that they practise within the law and receive appropriate training and support for the role.

Before making an application for detention the AMHP will have conducted a thorough assessment and consulted with the patient's 'nearest relative' (see below) and, where possible, professionals who know the individual. Their role is described as a statutory role (defined in law) and cannot be delegated. Local authorities provide a rota of to ensure 24-hour availability. Following the assessment the AMHP has to provide a report outlining why the assessment was necessary and their reasons for detaining or not detaining the patient. In making decisions about detention the AMHP must take into consideration other legislation, such as the Human Rights Act 1998 and deprivation of liberty safeguards under the Mental Capacity Act 2005.

In addition to their role of making the application for detention the AMHP also has to agree to patients being placed on a community treatment order (see above). They also have to agree to any CTO being revoked, and must provide reports for and attend a Mental Health Review Tribunal (MHRT).

MENTAL HEALTH REVIEW TRIBUNAL (MHRT)

The Mental Health Review Tribunal (MHRT) is the statutory body responsible for reviewing a patient's detention under the Mental Health Act. They have the ability to discharge patients from detention and also from community treatment orders (CTOs). In addition to reviewing whether a patient needs to remain, they are also responsible for the review of patients who are subject to a conditional discharge and CTO. The MHRT hears cases where an application has been made by a patient or the patient's nearest relative or they receive a referral from hospital managers or the Secretary of State.

The 2007 Mental Health Act amendments made a number of changes to the MHRT. England and Wales now have separate

MHRTs. The 2007 Act also introduced a two-tier tribunal system. Tier 1 hears the majority of cases while Tier 2 hears cases that are appealing Tier 1 decisions.

Within time periods specified by the MHA, detained patients and their nearest relatives have the right to appeal to the Mental Health Review Tribunal (MHRT) against further detention. With the power to discharge detained patients, the tribunal is a formal legal hearing and the patient has the right to request legal representation. The tribunal panel is appointed by the Lord Chancellor and consists of a lawyer, a medical member and a lay person.

RESPONSIBLE CLINICIAN AND APPROVED CLINICIAN

The 2007 amendments to the Mental Health Act changed much of the terminology used in the original Act. This included replacing the term Responsible Medical Officer (RMO) with Responsible Clinician (RC). This change in terminology has opened up the role to other disciplines such as nurses, occupational therapists and psychologists, although a doctor will still need to authorise detention.

The 2007 amendments have also specified that the professional taking the role of RC must possess a number of competencies, which include the assessment and management of risk and care planning.

The role of Approved Clinician (AC) is a new role specified within the 2007 amendments to the 1983 Mental Health Act. The Act does not specify that the role has to be filled by any one discipline but does stipulate that to fulfil the role of an AC the professional has to complete specialist training and demonstrate that they are 'competent' to take responsibility for treating people with mental disorder. When a clinician accepts the role of AC for a specific patient then they also become the Responsible Clinician.

Section 17: Planned and authorised leave from hospital

As part of a patient's treatment and discharge planning the multi-disciplinary team must assess how the patient will readjust to life in the community. Part of this assessment is made by the patient having periods of leave from the hospital. For patients who have been detained under sections 2, 3 or 37 (without restrictions) of the Mental Health Act this assessment is done by the patient having periods of section 17 leave away from the hospital. Section 17 leave can only be authorised by the Responsible Clinician following assessment by the multi-disciplinary team and is for specified periods of time building up to overnight leave. If the leave is for a period of longer than seven nights then the RC needs to consider if a CTO might be more appropriate.

Patients who are detained under section 37 with a section 41 restriction order cannot have section 17 leave without permission of the Secretary of State, and patients who are detained under sections 35, 36, 38, 47 and 48 (that part of the Act dealing with mentally disordered offenders) are not entitled to section 17 leave.

Section 117 aftercare

Under section 117, health trusts and social services have to provide aftercare to patients who have been detained and treated under sections 3, 37 (with or without restrictions) or 48 or 47 of the Mental Health Act. It includes patients who are subject to CTOs. Section 117 responsibilities continue even after the patient has been discharged from the section that detained them in hospital. The decision to discharge section 117 responsibilities is a joint decision between health and social care agencies and can only be made when both agree that there are no longer any ongoing health or social care needs.

All patients receiving specialist mental health services must be registered under the Care Programme Approach (see Chapter 2) and be assigned a 'care co-ordinator'. When patients are discharged from hospital the care plan must specify the required aftercare arrangements. For patients who are subject to section 117, the care plan has to be agreed by the relevant statutory services. Through section 117 arrangements, funding can be requested to enable the delivery of care (such as appropriate accommodation, work retraining or further education) identified in the care plan.

COMMUNITY TREATMENT ORDERS

Patients who have been detained under section 3 of the MHA can, following an assessment of their needs and Care Programme Approach requirements, also be made subject to a CTO after they have been discharged. The CTO can specify that their discharge is dependent on them complying with certain conditions, such as taking medication and keeping appointments with the mental health team. If the patient fails to comply with their conditions they can be recalled to hospital for up to 72 hours. If at the end of that time the clinical team decides to revoke the CTO, the patient's detention is re-started as if they had been newly assessed under section 3 of the MHA. They are also automatically referred to a Mental Health Review Tribunal.

Compulsory admission to hospital

Part II of the Mental Health Act is concerned with hospital admissions and guardianship, and describes the more familiar sections (often referred to as the 'civil sections') of the Act under which 90 per cent of detained patients are admitted (Department of Health 2002–2003). Part II of the Act allows a patient to be compulsorily admitted under the Act where this is necessary:

- in the interests of his/her own health or

- in the interests of his/her own safety or

- for the protection of other people.

The table opposite outlines the most commonly used admission sections under Part II of the Mental Health Act 1983.

Table 7.1: Part II of the Mental Health Act – key sections

SECTION	PURPOSE	REQUIREMENTS	GROUNDS FOR DETENTION	DURATION
2	Admission for assessment	An application based on two medical recommendations, one of which must be from a section 12 doctor.	The patient must be suffering from a mental disorder of a nature and degree that requires the patient to be detained in hospital in the interests of his/her own safety or for the protection of the general public.	28 days
3	Treatment	An application and two medical recommendations, one of which must be made by a section 12 doctor. If possible one doctor must have had previous acquaintance of the patient. Both doctors must have seen the patient within five days of each other and admission must be within 14 days.	That the patient is suffering from a mental disorder as defined in the Mental Health Act. In addition the disorder must be of a nature or degree that requires the patient to be detained in hospital in the interest of his/her safety or for the protection of the public. The 2007 Amendments to the Mental Health Act introduced the 'appropriate treatment test', which means that medical treatment can be provided. The definition of medical treatment is broad and includes both psychological treatment and rehabilitation in addition to drug treatments. The patient can be treated against their will for the first three months but cannot be given ECT against their will without assessment by a Second Opinion Appointed Doctor (SOAD).	Initially 6 months. If further detention is required the section can be renewed initially for six months then annually up to one year

cont.

SECTION	PURPOSE	REQUIREMENTS	GROUNDS FOR DETENTION	DURATION
4	Emergency admission for assessment	One application based on one medical recommendation made by either a doctor who knows the patient or a section 12 doctor. The applicant and doctor must have seen the patient within 24 hours of each other and the patient must be admitted within 24 hours.	For extreme emergencies where a patient's condition warrants immediate admission and there is insufficient time to arrange a second medical recommendation, which would cause 'undesirable delay' – the reason for using section 4 must be clearly stated. Emergency treatment can be given if the patient is assessed as not having capacity, in which case treatment can be given against their will.	72 hours
5(2)	Application in respect of a patient already in hospital – doctor's holding power	A doctor who is the patient's doctor or nominated deputy. The doctor must provide the hospital managers with a report justifying the reason for detention.	For the legal detention of a patient who wants to leave hospital but is assessed as not well enough to do so.	72 hours – this is considered sufficient time to assess the patient and for an application for section 2 or 3 to be made.
5(4)	Application in respect of a patient already in hospital – nurse's holding power	A first level nurse (RMN). The nurse must record in writing the conditions for the detention and provide the hospital managers with a report as to why detention was necessary.	To prevent an informal patient from leaving the ward if there is evidence that the patient is suffering from a mental disorder and detention is necessary for the patient's safety or the safety of the public. Only to be used if it is not possible for a doctor to immediately attend the ward.	Six hours, during which time the patient must be examined by a doctor. The detention ends when the doctor arrives on the ward. The time section 5(4) was applied must be noted because if the doctor decides to apply section 5(2) the 72 hours starts from when the section 5(4) was applied.

Patients concerned in criminal proceedings

Part III of the MHA applies to prisoners or those involved in criminal proceedings, and can apply to remand and sentenced prisoners. Table 7.2 on the following page gives a brief explanation of the most commonly used sections for this patient group, although there are several more that have not been included as they are generally applied in specialist settings such as secure units and special hospitals and are beyond the remit of this book.

Table 7.2: Part III of the Mental Health Act – key sections

SECTION	PURPOSE	REQUIREMENTS	GROUNDS FOR DETENTION	DURATION AND RIGHTS
37	Enables the court to send an offender to hospital for treatment	Can be imposed at either the magistrates or crown court. In the case of the magistrates court the court only has to be satisfied that the offender committed the offence for which they are accused. In the crown court the offender has to be convicted. The hospital have to agree to admit the patient within 28 days.	The court must be satisfied on the evidence of two doctors, one of whom is section 12 approved, that the offender is suffering from a mental disorder as defined in the Act.	Initially six months. Can be renewed for a further six months and then annually. During the first six months neither the patient nor their nearest relative has a right to appeal to the MHRT.
41	A restriction order can only be applied to section 37. It is not a standalone section	Only the crown court can apply a restriction order once a person has been convicted of an offence punishable by imprisonment. A magistrates court can refer a case to the crown court for a restriction order to be applied. The RMO has to agree to provide the Home Office with reports of the patient's progress at least once a year. The patient cannot leave hospital without the permission of the Home Office.	As for section 37 plus the court must take into consideration: the nature of the offence; the person's criminal history; the risk of the person committing further offences; and protecting the public from serious harm.	With or without limit of time. The patient can apply to an MHRT between six and 12 months from the order being made, and then every subsequent 12 months. The Home Office must approve all periods of leave based on the current risk assessment.

47	Transfer to hospital of sentenced prisoners	Transfer has to take place within 14 days of the order being made.	The criteria are the same as for sections under Part II of the Act and section 37 with the added criterion that the Home Office is of the opinion that transfer is necessary having first considered the interests of the public.	No limit of time. Transfer comes to an end on the earliest date that the patient could have been released from prison if they had not been transferred to hospital. However, if the person still requires detention after this date, they automatically become reclassified as a 'notional section 37'.
49	A restriction order that the Home Office can apply to section 47			No limit of time. If the patient no longer requires hospital treatment the Home Office has to be informed so that the patient can be returned to prison.

The Mental Capacity Act 2005 ─────────────

The Mental Capacity Act 2005 protects people who cannot make decisions for themselves. This may include people with a variety of mental health problems, although it should be stressed that even severe mental illness is not necessarily a barrier to the ability to make decisions about one's life and care.

The MCA principles

The MCA is governed by five core principles. These can be summarised as follows:

- Every adult has the right to make their own decisions if they have the capacity to do so. As staff working with mentally ill service users, we assume capacity unless presented with very clear evidence that the person is not able to make decisions for themselves.

- People sometimes struggle to make decisions for themselves, but often *can* do so with empathy and good communication skills on the part of staff.

- Service users sometimes make decisions which seem alarming or unsafe to those working with them. This isn't evidence of absent capacity. People have, under the MCA, the right to make their own decisions unless we have very strong evidence to try and prevent them from doing so.

- Any act done for, or any decision made on behalf of, someone who lacks capacity must be in their best interests.

- Any act done for, or any decision made on behalf of, someone who lacks capacity should be the least restrictive option possible.

Training for health and social care staff is compulsory, and we advise readers to use the resources highlighted below for a much more detailed review of how the Act, and mental capacity as a whole, affect people with mental disorders.

The Deprivation of Liberty Safeguards (DoLS)

Again this can be an important yet complex area, which we suggest warrants training and more detailed research appropriate to readers' workplace and situation. Essentially, if someone such as a nursing home resident has been deemed as lacking capacity, the DoLS determines a pathway by which the 'decision maker' such as a manager or person in charge must apply for local authority authorisation to deprive that person of their liberty. A deprivation of liberty that has not been validly authorised will be illegal.

References

HSCIC (2014) *Inpatients Formally Detained in Hospitals under the Mental Health Act 1983, and Patients Subject to Supervised Community Treatment: Annual Report, England, 2013/14.* Leeds: Health and Social Care Information Centre.

Further Reading

Graham, M. and Cowley, J. (2015) *A Practical Guide to the Mental Capacity Act 2015.* London and Philadelphia, PA: Jessica Kingsley Publishers.

Jones, R. (2014) *Mental Health Act Manual.* London: Sweet & Maxwell.

HSCIC (2012) *Mental Capacity Act Deprivation of Liberty Safeguards Collection.* Leeds: Health and Social Care Information Centre.

MIND (undated) *The Mind Guide to the Mental Health Act 1983.* London: MIND.

SUBJECT INDEX

AUTHOR INDEX